FLORIDA HOSPITAL *Healthcare & Leadership* MONOGR...

MONOGRAPH VOLUME V

Holding on to What is Sacred

HOW TO PROTECT ORGANIZATIONAL VALUES AND ENHANCE MISSION VITALITY

RANDY HAFFNER, PhD, MBA

FLORIDA HOSPITAL

Since 1908

FLORIDA HOSPITAL
HEALTHCARE
& LEADERSHIP
MONOGRAPH SERIES

HOLDING ON TO WHAT IS SACRED
Copyright © 2010 Randy Haffner
Monograph Volume 5
Published by Florida Hospital
683 Winyah Drive, Orlando, Florida 32803

TO EXTEND *the* HEALTH *and* HEALING MINISTRY *of* CHRIST

GENERAL EDITOR	Todd Chobotar
WRITER	Steven Mosley
EXTERNAL PEER REVIEW	Mike Toupin
	Rick Stiffney
	Chris Thomason
INTERNAL PEER REVIEW	Ted Hamilton, MD, MBA
	Peter Bath, DMin
	Sy Saliba, PhD
	Brian Paradis
PROMOTION	Stephanie Rick, MBA
PRODUCTION	Lillian Boyd
COPY EDITOR	Barbara Trombitas
PHOTOGRAPHY	Spencer Freeman
COVER DESIGN	BONDesign
INTERIOR DESIGN	The Herman Lewis Design Syndicate

Cataloging-in-Publication Data for this monograph
is available from the Library of Congress
ISBN 13: 978-0-9820409-7-3
ISBN 10: 0-9820409-7-0

Printed in the United States of America
FP 10 9 8 7 6 5 4 3 2 1

For volume discounts please contact special sales at:
HealthProducts@FLHosp.org | 407-303-1929

For more resources on Whole Person Health please visit:
FloridaHospitalPublishing.com

CONTENTS

EDITOR'S INTRODUCTION

AUTHOR CHARLES STANLEY ONCE WROTE, "There is an unseen current that we all battle everyday—a current that leads to a certain destruction...We have a tendency to drift toward that on which we have focused our attention." True for organizations as well as individuals. If we don't stay focused on what matters most, we end up somewhere we didn't intend.

Perhaps that's the reason I'm so excited about this monograph. In the following pages Dr. Randy Haffner lays out a persuasive vision for how organizations can stay focused on their true values so they don't end up somewhere they never intended.

Three years ago I got a sneak peek at this manuscript and knew Dr. Haffner was onto something special. At the time his research and ideas were being developed for his doctoral dissertation. But I immediately felt they deserved a wider audience than most academic research papers receive. So I started talking with him about publishing it in some form after completion. Three years later, it's ready to go. I believe Dr. Haffner has done an exceptional job of distilling his research into an accessible and practical tool for business professionals.

The most intriguing aspect of the manuscript to me is Dr. Haffner's concept of Confessional Identity—a term he coined to delineate a company's core convictions. Confessional Identity pinpoints the very essence of mission. It transcends trendy corporate speak and seeks the spiritual heart of an organization's reason for being.

If you work in the corporate world, you need to read this. And if you work for a not-for-profit, faith-based organization I believe this should be mandatory reading for everyone on your team. Why? Because so much is at stake. Your employees need to know why you exist and why their efforts matter. Your customers need to know why you really care. Your leaders need to embrace your core convictions whole-heartedly or they will lose direction.

In today's business environment it's far too easy to focus on short-term gains at the expense of your Confessional Identity. Don't let this happen to you. Learn instead the secret of *Holding on to What is Sacred*.

Todd Chobotar, General Editor

FOREWORD

ORGANIZATIONS THAT EXIST SOLELY TO MAKE MONEY will eventually fail; those that succeed in the long-term pursue a higher calling – something more than just the creation of wealth. The Great Recession of 2008-09 illustrated for most of the developed world the ultimate fate and cost of business driven by unbridled greed.

Dr. Haffner's prescient study recognizes that a successful service organization is not adequately defined by its balance sheet alone. Rather, his work probes for the soul of an organization and the real values that the customers recognize as integral to the products and services delivered. He then proceeds to suggest measurements that can complement the financial section of the organization's scorecard with measures pertinent to the health of the organization's soul.

While his study is written to not-for-profit organizations – and more specifically faith-based organizations – the methodology in his case study of Florida Hospital is relevant for the for-profit world as well. All businesses have values that the employees learn and live by. The values may not be deliberately identified. They may not be contributing positively to success. There may even be competing value systems in different parts of the organization. Haffner emphasizes the importance of understanding the values, managing around a common set of values, and then living them throughout the organization.

Values that drive a successful organization should not change. Strategies and tactics change with the developments of technology, markets and society over time. But values are the bedrock of the organization. Haffner will help readers probe the essence of the bedrock of their organizations.

Kent Seltman, Ph.D., M.B.A.

Rochester, MN

Co-author, *Management Lessons from Mayo Clinic: Inside One of the World's Most Admired Service Organizations*, McGraw-Hill 2008

THE CASE FOR CONFESSIONAL IDENTITY:
A REFLECTION OF YOUR MISSION

THE LETTER INSTANTLY CAPTURED MY ATTENTION. It wasn't because it bore an impressive embossed letterhead; it was written on a plain piece of paper. It wasn't because it came from a person of authority or influence; the letter was penned by a complete stranger, a woman named Mabel. It wasn't because it was the only letter I received that day. No, it lay in the middle of a stack of mail on top of my desk.

At the time I was busy assessing the environment and culture of Porter Adventist Hospital in Denver, Colorado, caught up in my first 100 days at a new work place – after 19 years halfway across the country at Florida Hospital. So of course I eagerly absorbed perspectives from anyone and everyone who could give me insights about Porter.

But despite being immersed in a lot of new information, this letter just grabbed me. Perhaps it was Mabel's handwriting. The unsteady hand that wrote it clearly belonged to a person advanced in years. Perhaps it was the first line that described how she had been a patient at Porter Adventist Hospital the previous year – from Thanksgiving all the way until Christmas. Those five weeks had been spent in an acute care setting. That's a very long time to be in the hospital. And it gave Mabel a lot of experiences to reflect on the environment and culture of this institution.

Reading the letter intently, I learned of her days in the Intensive Care Unit, followed by a stint on the medical floor. She described the tests and procedures including many echograms, x-rays, CT scans and having her heart and lungs "drained three times." And she kept mentioning individuals by name – associates on our staff whom she wanted to thank, people she actually felt close to. Then one line stopped me in my tracks: "Every day and every experience was a reflection of your mission statement."

I leaned back in my chair. What a statement from someone who had taken a good look at us for forty difficult days, plenty of time to notice every little wrinkle and quirk of an organization. The questions began burning in my head. How do you create a culture in which the mission of an organization is lived every work week? How do you maintain that kind of environment year after year? Is it possible for a experience like

Mabel's to be replicated each day, through every interaction with every employee?

After all, no group of human beings is perfect. No organization is perfect. Mabel couldn't help ending her letter with a little tongue-in-cheek postscript, "Steaks should not be hockey pucks."

THE FAILING ENTERPRISE

WHEN I GREW UP IN THE 1970's, most products of inferior quality were stamped with the label: "Made in Japan". Fast forward a few decades and you find that Japanese electronics and automobiles are regarded as some of the finest technological products in the world. What propelled such a dramatic turnaround? Most point to one man who played a key role: Dr. W. Edwards Deming, an American statistician, professor and consultant. He'd been making discoveries about quality control and process improvement in the United States, but was unable to find a receptive audience among manufacturers here. So, he turned his attention to Japan and found a ready welcome. After he assisted Japan in improving its products for a while, Dr. Deming looked back to the U.S. and saw us still laboring under old procedures and standards. He issued a warning that proved ominously predictive: Despite worldwide manufacturing dominance, "Survival is not mandatory."[1]

In recent years we've had to grapple with the near collapse of the American automobile industry. Companies like General Motors and Chrysler, once looked upon as invincible titans, find themselves on the brink of extinction. And much more than Detroit has been shaken. Among businesses in America, bankruptcy rates increased dramatically. We have all seen businesses that were at one point thriving but find themselves in the unfortunate reality that the only remaining option is to close their doors. Yes, Dr. Deming, survival is not mandatory.

That leaves us with a very big question: why do some enterprises flourish while others fail? The prevailing literature suggests there is a bottom line when it comes to preserving the bottom line. Organizations can sustain vitality and longevity by doing two things: promoting adaptive innovations and preserving core convictions.

For the long-term vitality of any organization, it will be essential to adapt to the times. Continuing to promote and introduce new products, techniques and approaches to be relevant in the marketplace is essential. Most thriving companies have devoted millions, if not billions, of dollars annually to understand their market in the pursuit of innovation and product development. For the most part, there is a good amount of information known and available on this first component.

But what about that second component: preserving core convictions? What is known on this topic?

DISCOVERING YOUR CORE IDEOLOGY

ONE STUDY CONDUCTED BY JIM COLLINS AND JERRY PORRAS, former professors at Stanford University's Graduate School of Business, evaluated the performance of various companies over a 50-year period. It put a spotlight on 18 of the most successful companies. And here's what they found. Seventeen of those top 18 companies were guided by a certain ideology. What kind? One deeply rooted in meaningful values that transcend mere profitability.[2]

Here's how Collins and Porras explain it: "A deeply held core ideology gives a company both a strong sense of identity and a thread of continuity that holds the organization together in the face of change."[3]   What is core ideology? These researchers define it as the combination of core values and organizational purpose. And they further clarify what these two essential components are about. Core values are "the organization's essential and enduring tenets – a small set of general guiding principles; not to be confused with specific cultural or operating practices; not to be compromised for financial gain or short-term expediency." Purpose is "the organization's fundamental reasons for existence beyond just making money – a perpetual guiding star on the horizon; not to be confused with specific goals or business strategies."[4]

Core ideology is essential, we are told. It's not just fluff on a corporate portfolio. Nor is this simply a recipe that can be copied from company to company. As Collins and Parras explain, "Our research indicates that the authenticity of the ideology and the extent to which a company attains consistent alignment with the ideology counts more than the *content* of the ideology."[5]

This idea of core ideology has actually been branded in various ways over the years. Some business researchers describe it as a culture, others as shared vision, moral purpose, or collaborative purpose. Regardless of the label used, the principle is the same. Organizational performance is measurably enhanced through a set of articulated convictions that are incorporated throughout the enterprise.

Another researcher, Peter Senge, gives us a useful insight on how this idea of shared vision relates to purpose and values. He writes, "a shared vision changes people's relationship with the company. It is no longer 'their company,' it becomes 'our company.' A shared vision is the first step in allowing people who mistrusted each other to begin to work together." According to Senge, shared vision creates a common identity.[6]

Michael Fullan, Dean of Education at the University of Toronto writes, "Businesses are realizing more and more that having moral purpose is critical to sustainable success."[7] And students of the corporate world have begun zeroing in on this fact: sustaining vitality is not a destination as much as an ongoing journey. On this journey, Collins and Porras remind us, "ultimately, the only thing a company should not change over time is its core ideology."[8]

Importantly, core ideology is more than just a statement of vision and values. Noted author and speaker Margaret Wheatley suggests, "Values, vision, ethics – these are too soft, too ethereal, to serve as management tools."[9] She explains that if people are guided by a compelling purpose, the whole system will create great coherence that's even more orderly than something dished out by a controlling management culture. In other words, while vision and values are important, purpose and core convictions provide the raison d'être for an organization.

So there you have it. Various authors have all focused on this organizational set of beliefs and mission. They use different labels: Purpose, Core Convictions, Core Ideology, Collaborative Purpose. But they're talking about the same essential thing. And that's what I'm going to focus on, especially as it relates to the social sector of not-for-profit organizations. Although my field of expertise for some decades now has been within the healthcare field, the implications and lessons are applicable across a range of faith-based and non-profit organizations.

In examining the challenges of non-profits, I will use the term "confessional identity." It's not a phrase used in the popular press. Confessional identity connotes a different level of purpose that transcends the cursory and touches on the sacred, the spiritual. For some who first hear this term, there is a discomfort and confusion that is attributed to the more common definition of confession, which is disclosing one's sins. But there is another definition that highlights the act of the public profession of an individual's or an organization's sacred beliefs that is the intended use here. Rather than simply describing what an organization does, confessional identity identifies the very essence of who an organization is.

THE PLIGHT OF THE NOT-FOR-PROFIT

WE HAVE AN ABUNDANCE OF LITERATURE that zeroes in on the dynamics of publicly traded, for-profit businesses. Not-for-profit organizations, however, typically suffer from a scarcity of hard data. In fact, Jim Collins quickly determined this reality after completing his national best-selling book *Good to Great*, and then published a monograph to give guidance to the social sector.[10] Without better options, most charitable organizations simply try to force-fit good business practices into their day-to-day operations. But those principles don't always gain traction particularly in light of the larger concept of confessional identity.

Many times, the not-for-profit organization has a tough time gauging its actual success or its organizational standing. In the for-profit corporate world, success can be measured pretty easily. Financial profitability, market share, and market capitalization can be reduced to clear numbers. On most occasions, one knows if bankruptcy is looming.

But how is that different for the not-for-profit? From a pure financial perspective, many of the realities are the same. One must have a healthy balance sheet and a business model in which revenues exceed expenses. However, the not-for-profits ascribe to a higher purpose than mere financial stability. For a not-for-profit, there is a confessional identity that can be much trickier to quantify and measure. Because of this, the confessional identity of organizations can be at risk without even knowing it. To borrow from Deming, confessional identity survival is not mandatory. You may have a very functional business model, but how do you know if you are fully functioning, truly advancing your confessional identity?

Given this environment, many not-for-profits simply don't exercise the level of discipline and leadership that is required to realize their purpose and destiny. That's unfortunate for several reasons.

> The truth is not-for-profits have a lot to offer the general business world. When their confessional identity is correctly conceived and actualized, they model the best way for any business to remain vital in the long term. The not-for-profit segment has the potential to create a higher purpose that transcends the tyranny of immediate financial returns, the exclusivity of financial metrics or shareholders investments. Contained within the confessional identity is that higher purpose and calling. That is an ideology worth pursuing. It can take us to another level.

Some research keys on that point. Kent Miller, Professor of Strategic Management at Michigan State University, suggests that faith-based organizations maintain vitality by "reaffirming traditional beliefs while continuously adapting their expression to environmental conditions."[11] Industries mutate. Companies evolve. Given that fact, Collins and Porras tell us it is the core ideology that functions as a "bonding glue and guiding force that holds a visionary company together."[12] They further state that "the visionary companies don't merely declare an ideology; they also take steps to make the ideology pervasive throughout the organization and transcend any individual leader."[13]

Many people don't realize that the vast majority of higher education and hospital entities in the United States of America were founded as faith-based institutions by a religious order or sponsoring church entity. These institutions began with a confessional identity that reflected the spiritual worldview of their religious sponsor. However, things change over time. That confessional identity often wears down and unknowingly evaporates. Quite a few big-name institutions like Harvard University, Yale University and Princeton have discarded the core ideology that played such a key role in their beginning. Some give practical reasons, some philosophical ones. But the reality is that the distinctive confessional identity just doesn't exist anymore.

And that presents a problem. Chun Wei Choo, Faculty of Information Studies at the University of Toronto writes, "More than ever, organizations are keenly aware that their ability to survive and evolve is determined by their capacity to make sense of or influence their environments and to constantly renew meaning and purpose in light of new conditions."[14]

A COROLLARY ON HIGHER EDUCATION

A T SOME POINT, MOST INSTITUTIONS RUN INTO a tension between trying to adapt to a changing environment and trying to preserve a confessional identity. Unfortunately, many have not been able to do both. Most of us have either lived in that tension or have witnessed it first-hand. Stories are often shared about how some organizations have clung to their ideals without regard for their market realities. Others have simply discarded their founding values in order to pursue new opportunities.

> In the formative years in the United States, nearly all universities and hospitals were created by Christian orders and churches for the purposes of ministry formation and outreach. The vast majority of these universities and hospitals have severed all formal relationships with their founding religious entities. The sanctity of that core religious heritage, so formative in the early years, has simply been discarded, diminished or increasingly less relevant.

The published information regarding this topic and hospitals is scarce, but abundant when it comes to institutions of higher learning. In one historical review, James Burtchaell—one of the early presidents of the American Academy of Religion— outlined the gradual disengagement of various colleges and universities originally associated with Congregationalist, Presbyterian, Methodist, Baptist, Lutheran, Catholic and Evangelical denominations.[15] There's no single pattern to all this. But there are general themes that run through both their founding and their loss of confessional identity.

It was clergymen who commonly orchestrated the beginnings of institutions of higher learning in the U.S. People saw the need for advanced education in order to create a stable new nation – and a stable church. George Marsden, a professor of History at the University of Notre Dame, gives us a striking picture of how closely the development of higher education was tied to the development of the United States of America. Our founding fathers and mothers believed that the establishment of a civilized society required the presence of educational opportunities. Marsden writes: "Next to religion, education was the best means of taming an unruly populace and assimilating diverse peoples into a common culture with shared ideals. Education would develop the individual sense of duty and a national conscience."[16]

These educational opportunities were established through various sectarian Protestant and Catholic churches. Remarkably, only six years after the founding of the first Puritan settlement in Massachusetts, these Protestant pilgrims began the work of establishing the educational entity that would become Harvard University. In Harvard's first 100 years, the majority of its graduates were trained as clergy.

Later, as Americans focused on the goal of establishing a civil society, they wrestled with the challenge of reconciling sectarian belief with secular interests. At first, people took comfort from the fact that secular and sacred interests could both be fulfilled within the same university setting. However, in the 18th century, Thomas Jefferson led an effort to separate control of America's universities from specific sectarian church organizations. At the time, the issue was not so much the involvement of religious organizations in higher education, but rather the particular sectarian beliefs of specific denominations being propagated in colleges and universities with "public" monies. That conflict ultimately made its way before the United States Supreme Court. The court ruled for the immunity of charitable corporations from state control. Many universities with a denominational affiliation continued to receive government funding in the nineteenth century.

Despite the denominational ties of these institutions, students were welcome regardless of their faith professions. In the early years, the university President was required to be a member of the sponsoring denomination. The relationship between the university and the church usually involved how students were provided for and how the operation was sustained financially. However, as students not associated with the denomination enrolled in these universities and other funding sources became available, the dependence on the sponsoring denomination was significantly marginalized. Burtchaell explains that "for some colleges, effective emancipation came in the form of a sudden, large benefactor."[17]

Along with these newfound funding options, the alumni began to assume more leadership on the Boards of Trustees and gradually replaced clergy and church leaders. At the same time, the president and faculty felt increasingly "confined, stifled or trivialized by their church affiliation."[18] As faculty members developed their expertise within given fields, their primary devotion began to focus on their careers, their professional status, rather than the institution and its confessional identity. Over time, the faculty devolved from active membership in the church to actual intolerance. They began to view their religious affiliation as something that prohibited unadulterated freedom in the search for academic truth. In essence, the core conviction of academic truth trumped their confessional identity.

In those days, theories associated with Darwinism were sweeping through the scientific community, and that seemed to challenge the very fabric of many universities' biblical declarations. Positivism also began to throw its weight around. That exclusive focus on the empirical, the measurable, appeared at odds with religious teachings. Robert Benne writes, "To the academic elite, these Christian enterprises seemed to be atavistic throwbacks to a bygone world. They seemed to be clinging to a way of understanding the world that had been surpassed by a new and more successful faith."[19] The first victim of that "new faith" in many universities was straightforward sectarian teachings. Moral philosophy replaced theology as the primary curriculum for principled scholarship. Higher learning in America had taken a set course toward methodical secularization.

Those on the cutting edge of this new direction tended to be progressive professors. They claimed that beliefs tied to a university's church connection stifled academic freedom. They advocated for an institution in which "intellectual freedom is honored far above orthodoxy."[20] George Marsden further elaborates:

The fatal weakness in conceiving of the university as a broadly Christian institution was its higher commitments to scientific and professional ideals and to the demand for a unified public life. In the light of such commitments academic expression of Christianity seemed at best superfluous and at worst unscientific and unprofessional. Most of those associated with higher education were still Christian, but in academic life, as in so many other parts of modern life, religion would increasingly be confined to private spheres.[21]

There were also external factors which contributed to these internal scholastic shifts. Governmental and private foundations funding sources like the Carnegie Foundation for the Advancement of Teaching actually specified that a school could not remain under church influence if it was to be eligible for grants and financial support.

Looking back we can see that churches did express concern about this path to secularism. However, they usually did so a decade after it was already functionally in place at a given institution. As Burtchaell explains, "Later, worship and moral behavior were easily set aside because no one could imagine they had anything to do with learning."[22] Necessary funding was arriving independently of the church. So was the student body in general, so these higher educational institutions allowed the relationship with the church to "atrophy" into a more principled indifference.

> Interestingly enough, today we do find something different rising in the American landscape: institutions consciously standing in stark contrast to this disengagement of faith from learning.

One of the most prominent is Baylor University in Waco, Texas. In its ten-year vision document entitled "Baylor 2012," the President and CEO, Robert B. Sloan Jr., boldly declared, "We aspire to what few institutions, if any, have ever achieved – recognition both as a top tier university and as an institution committed to Christ." Baylor University seeks to challenge the assumptions that led to the separation of some of the most respected universities and their sponsoring churches. In trying to reverse a very long course, Baylor states, "It is a legacy of modern thought to believe that the pathway divides between the uncompromised pursuit of intellectual excellence and intense faithfulness to the Christian tradition. We believe that the highest intellectual excellence is fully compatible with orthodox Christian devotion. Indeed, the two are not only compatible, but mutually reinforcing."

Baylor is very aware of the historical tension between a confession of religious truth and unfettered intellectual pursuits. It is careful to state that "all truth is open to inquiry." Acknowledging the sectarian challenges in the past, Baylor affirms:

> *Because the Church, the one truly democratic and multicultural community, is not identical with any denomination, we believe that Baylor will serve best, recruit more effectively, and both preserve and enrich its Baptist identity more profoundly, if we draw our faculty, staff, and students from the full range of Christian traditions.*[23]

In the two years since adopting the strategic initiative of Baylor 2012, this university has taken significant steps toward achieving its vision. Each new faculty hire is assessed for her or his Christian commitment. Distinguished Christian scholars have been recruited; frequent seminars and panel discussions are orchestrated. Implementing this vision hasn't come without opposition. It took nearly two years for the Faculty Senate to officially adopt the plan. President and CEO, Robert Sloan Jr., recently resigned under intense pressure. Some question whether Baylor 2012 will ultimately succeed in fulfilling the dual aspiration of excellence in academics within a clearly Christian context.

Robert Benne, Director of the Center for Religion and Society at Roanoke College in Virginia, is one who has looked back on that long historical trend of so many church-founded colleges and universities breaking from their sponsoring religious entities. He comments on why: "A short and flippant answer to these questions is simply this: an adequate number of persons – board, administrators, faculty, and students – with a firm understanding of and commitment to the vision and ethos of each school's sponsoring heritage was not available to either school or church at the necessary times to translate that heritage into the

KEY THEMES

+ **Vision** – An Identified Confessional Identity that can reconcile the tensions

+ **Ethos** – Beliefs, Customs and Practices that support the Confessional Identity

+ **People** – Key Board, Leaders and Staff who could interpret and maintain the Confessional Identity

Table 1

school's life in a pervasive manner. Not enough committed and competent persons were present at crucial times to insist that the sponsoring heritage be publicly and fittingly relevant in all the facets of college life. That is the crux of the matter."[24]

Three themes are referenced here: a vision, an ethos, and Christian persons who honor and cherish the sponsoring faith (see Table 1). Benne uses "vision" in a way very similar to how I have identified "confessional identity" as a core ideology.

> Without principled intention, any faith-based institution could easily follow the well-traveled path of higher education. On that road, the requirements of a church can be perceived or realized as more problematic than beneficial. That course, however, can be reversed. To make that possible, I believe the three components identified by Benne are of crucial importance: vision, ethos and a careful selection of people who will support and enhance the vision are precisely what can protect and sustain our institutional confessional identity.

Benne shows the concentric nature of these three factors when he writes:

Without a public theological rationale for the ongoing legitimacy of a religious way of life on campus, that way of life tends to diminish over time. Further, without such a rationale for a continuing critical mass of persons from the sponsoring religious tradition, that critical mass tends to shrink as well. In a curious way, then, both religious ethos and the persons necessary to bring that ethos to bear are dependent upon an adequate theological vision of a school's identity and mission.[25]

We have gleaned insights from this historical look at institutions of higher learning. This information can now be used to create a principled method to analyze and assess the key factors that will determine the organizational attributes necessary to sustain an institution's confessional identity.

THE CONFESSIONAL IDENTITY MODEL: THE VALUES MATRIX

LET'S LOOK AT THE BIG PICTURE. To protect any confessional identity, an organization must focus on this: a method to assess and promote its core convictions. That's a necessity. For a conventional corporation, there's usually a plethora of tools and metrics available to assess the financial, regulatory and service aspects of a business. But the status of a confessional identity is much harder to evaluate. You can examine the ongoing operational health and welfare of your enterprise without too much difficulty. But the essential aspects of confessional identity can often be too ethereal to address with any consistency or certainty. That's why the following simple confessional identity matrix (Figure 1) can be an extremely helpful assessment tool. It has been developed to describe the relationship between the level of core conviction articulation and the wholistic adherence to those core convictions. In other words, it focuses on how well a confessional identity is expressed and how closely it is followed.

To understand the matrix, defining some key terms is necessary: Core Convictions are the essential elements, properties and purpose of an organization that sustain its confessional identity. I'm using the word wholistic in evaluating adherence, instead of the more common spelling, holistic, for a reason. Holistic is usually defined from a secular view as the interdependence of the parts to make a whole. The term wholistic refers more specifically to the intimate relationship of the mind, body, and spirit as dimensions of a singular reality. In other words, the mind, body and spirit are not simply three aspects that come together in a synergistic manner, but rather the three are dimensions of a whole.

Here's the basic premise of this matrix. In order to sustain the confessional identity of an organization, its core convictions must be well articulated and be wholistically applied. To have wholistic adherence, the vast majority of associates must understand the core convictions (mind), exhibit behaviors consistent with those core convictions on a daily basis (body) as well as have an emotional connection with the core convictions that brings meaning to the tasks at hand (spirit).

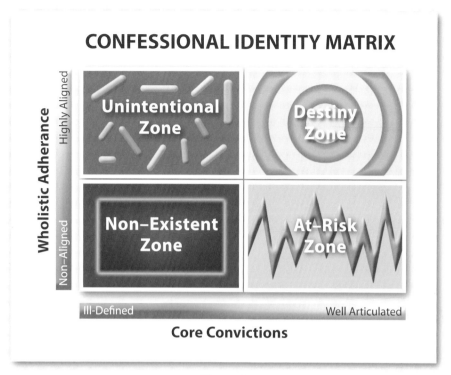

Figure 1

Let's apply these concepts to the matrix. Four basic possibilities follow:

- **Non-Existent Zone** – The state in which an organization has not defined its core convictions and associates show little or no wholistic adherence to them.

- **Unintentional Zone** – A state in which core convictions have not been well defined by the organization, but a strong organizational culture produces a tight alignment among the associates.

- **At-Risk Zone** – The state in which an organization has endeavored to define its core convictions but hasn't shown much wholistic adherence to them. The risk, involves losing or minimizing the organization's confessional identity.

- **Destiny Zone** – The status where an organization needs to be if its confessional identity is to be relevant and vibrant. In this state, core convictions are well articulated – cognitively, behaviorally and emotionally. In other words, mind, body and spirit all reinforce a single organizational reality.

The following case study will fully explore each of the four segments of the matrix from the standpoint of organizational theory. To illustrate the difference between each of these types of organizations, we will follow the experience of Nurse Nancy. Nancy is a composite figure based on the experience of many dedicated professional healthcare associates that I have known and spoken with over the past twenty years. While Nancy is characterized as a nurse and female, the experience is representative of many disciplines including therapists, pharmacists, technologists and other healthcare professionals of both genders.

Nurse Nancy is considering employment with several not-for-profit hospitals. She wants badly to work at a hospital with values that match her nursing ideals and that truly lives out its stated purpose. Unfortunately, it will take Nancy several attempts to find the perfect match, but her experience highlights the key differences between organizations. She will become a first-hand witness to the characteristics that distinguish organizations in the four quadrants of the Confessional Identity Matrix.

As she went through nursing school, Nancy was one of those people who took to heart the service ideals to which many others simply gave lip service. Marching down the aisle in her white gown at graduation, she worried a bit that she might be too idealistic. She'd heard plenty of stories from nurses who'd been simply worn down by the demands of the profession. But Nancy couldn't shake a hope lodged in her heart: there just had to be a Christian hospital out there somewhere that truly put the patient first and actively involved nurses in decisions about the clinical care process.

THE NON-EXISTENT ZONE

AS SHE TALKED WITH several fellow graduates, Nurse Nancy kept hearing about a new independent hospital that was just opening in town: Mercy Medical Center. The sign-on bonuses and wages were quite aggressive there compared to other medical facilities in the area. So she decided to check it out.

The facility proved to be absolutely breathtaking; it resembled a four-star hotel more than a hospital. As she talked with the personnel director there, Nurse Nancy got more and more excited. Surely here was an opportunity to be part of a new enterprise where she could grow in her career along with the hospital. And there were her student loans of course. The nice sign-on bonus and the promised increases in salary would come in handy. She'd even be able to get into a nice apartment right away! So Nancy signed on, with enthusiasm.

During orientation, however, she began to feel something was missing at Mercy. She did feel plenty of energy at the thought of finally putting all she'd learned during nursing school into practice. But, as she diligently took notes, listening to staff members cover various procedures, she found herself waiting for words that never came. What was it? Finally Nancy realized she was looking for some description of what the hospital stood for, what they were hoping to accomplish. Instead, all of the presentations seemed to focus on the details of risk management, fire safety, employee benefits and various regulatory requirements.

Nancy still hoped something might crystallize once she got on the cardiac unit. She kept quite busy. She tried to invest herself in these patients, some of whom were waiting for heart surgery. But a clear picture just didn't develop for her. Every morning when she walked into Mercy Medical Center she was reminded of what a spectacular building housed this enterprise. But nothing was ever discussed nor did Nancy ever witness behaviors by her fellow associates that created any connection to what that building actually stood for or what the hospital was really trying to accomplish. No one tried to make the "mercy" in Mercy Medical Center meaningful. It was just a name.

Nurse Nancy found herself wondering if she should seek a career elsewhere. She shook off the idea at first. The hospital had been established in a rapidly growing community. Its overall financial success was virtually assured. And yet the ambivalence about a higher calling or purpose haunted her. Why did core convictions at this place seem to be non-existent? Was there really a point to all her hard work? After nine months at Mercy, and several sleepless nights, she decided to look for employment elsewhere.

THE UNINTENTIONAL ZONE

IN THE FOLLOWING WEEKS, Nurse Nancy decided to get on several websites and look at other hospitals in the area. Surely she'd find a good place where she could have a satisfying career. She began to focus on the largest and most well-established hospital in the city, Union Hospital. All that Nancy read indicated the institution had achieved a well-respected stature in the community. She applied for a position. Given the national shortage of nurses, Nancy was quickly hired, despite her limited experience and short tenure with the previous employer.

As Nurse Nancy followed her assigned preceptor for the first two months, she was duly impressed. Nursing practices at Union seemed to have been well developed. There was clearly an established way of doing patient care at this place. Nancy wanted to be a part of this; she wanted to fit in. Wouldn't it be great to grow into a well-respected, seasoned nurse here!

After completing her preceptor training, Nurse Nancy happily settled into the routines of work in the Labor & Delivery Unit. Several years went by; Nancy helped bring hundreds of babies into the world, safe and whole. And yes, she appreciated the established, consistent way of doing things.

But again, something began to bother her. It hit her during a particular department meeting. The leadership covered a lot of material that was mostly about the details of running the unit. But no one spoke about the direction of the Labor & Delivery Unit, about overall goals, about how it fit into the mission of Union Hospital. Instead, after meetings, the staff would simply discuss various functions and make decisions regarding policies and procedures or technological advancements. It felt a little like an inadvertent and unintentional way of doing things. They looked at details, over and over; they hammered out "standard operating procedure," but no one talked about this in the context of long-term consequence or organizational direction. There didn't seem to be any real "union" in what the hospital was doing. No one was able to provide a rationale for their behaviors, their purpose and direction. At Union Hospital, there seemed to be a definitive practice without a professed purpose.

Although the Labor & Delivery Unit proved a pretty comfortable work setting for Nurse Nancy, after three years she felt compelled to look elsewhere. She still longed for a sense of fulfillment in a calling. She still dreamed of a place that really focused on the patient, an environment that allowed nurses to work with leadership to create a superior work environment while pursuing a higher calling.

THE AT-RISK ZONE

NURSE NANCY WAS SURE SHE FOUND the perfect hospital to work at shortly thereafter at Community Heights Health. At orientation she noted that the Chief Executive Officer spent three hours tracing the origins of the hospital for the new employees. He explained how that translated into the specific behaviors and values that were to be embraced by every associate. As she made her way down to the cafeteria, she was struck by the way various posters and artwork celebrated the hospital's core values. Nancy was even pleased to read the hospital's mission statement and core values – spelled out on the back of her employee badge. These people really did want to spotlight the sanctity of this institution's purpose.

The first several months proved rather blissful for Nurse Nancy at Community Heights Health. But gradually she found herself looking for signs that people were actually committed to the hospital's stated values. They seemed hard to come by. A notorious cardiovascular surgeon grew very angry about an honest mistake in scheduling that meant a delay of 45 minutes before starting his first case. After the surgeon threw a hallway tantrum, the director and administrator came down to confront him. But they quickly backed down when he threatened to take his cases elsewhere unless the scheduler was fired.

Days later Nurse Nancy found out that this scheduler, a woman with an unblemished record, had been reassigned away from the operating room. Nancy flashed back on one of the core values that had been emphasized by the CEO at orientation. Respect was supposed to be a big deal at Community Heights Health.

It was plastered on hallway posters and highlighted on every employee badge. The incident certainly seemed to clash with that stated value.

But Nancy didn't want to jump to conclusions. Surely the high purpose this hospital proclaimed would show up somewhere. She continued to carry out her nursing duties with an upbeat spirit and hopeful outlook. But one afternoon, a couple of the more seasoned nurses sat down with Nancy in the break room and offered to educate her about the way things really worked around the hospital. The two explained that there were two sets of reality at the hospital: what was officially proclaimed and what was actually practiced. While the hospital had aimed at certain ideals in the past, they said, its true agenda in the present was much more about financial success than the best care of patients.

Still, Nurse Nancy found it hard to give up on this idea of a high calling at Community Heights Health. Maybe these nurses were just two sour apples in an otherwise healthy orchard. So Nancy continued to serve her patients in the manner consistent with the values espoused by the organization.

But then months turned to years. Incidents turned into patterns. And Nancy had to face the fact that the hospital was consistently inconsistent. Yes, they emphasized certain values, but the application of those values remained spotty at best. There was clearly a lack of alignment between what the organization professed compared to what was practiced; a lack of realness and organizational integrity. Disenchantment began to set in.

By this time, Nurse Nancy had fallen in love and gotten married. Her husband landed a job in a neighboring state which necessitated a move. Having had experience now in three different settings, she was quite apprehensive about what to expect in their new town. Yes, Community Heights Health had shown more promise than the two previous institutions, but there was still quite a distance from the lofty core values someone might espouse and the application in her day-to-day work. Nancy felt like she'd experienced yet another disappointment.

THE DESTINY ZONE

AFTER SETTLING INTO HER FIRST house with her husband in their new town, Nurse Nancy began looking around for suitable employment. In considering the two hospital systems there, she ultimately chose Destiny Hospital. The basis for her decision was simple. Something became very clear as she watched the pre-employment video there and participated in the behavior-based interviews conducted by staff from the Intensive Care Unit where she would be working. This place was determined to hire only those who would be committed to the mission and core values of Destiny Hospital.

To be sure, orientation didn't seem that different from orientation at Community Heights Health. The Chief Executive Officer spent significant time tracing Destiny Hospital's history, mission, vision and values. And similarly, banners in the hallway spotlighted those values, as did the back of the associate badge. There were moments when Nancy felt a tug toward cynicism – she had already been down this path. She had learned that it wasn't hard for an institution to say all the right words. But Nancy decided to keep her mind open and her hope alive.

Being a more seasoned nurse, she quickly availed herself of the unofficial orientation that comes in the staff lounge and around cafeteria lunch tables. It was there that other nurses talked about the way things really happened at Destiny Hospital. Nancy listened carefully. These people actually spoke about how the hospital's values played out in their daily work life. They talked about how these values impacted their whole work environment in a positive way. In a sense, the mission and values seemed to be embedded in her co-workers as a natural extension of their character. Nancy had to take a deep breath. Had she finally found a real place where she could fulfill a high calling?

Last time I checked, Nurse Nancy continues to be a valued part of the Destiny Hospital team. And the fact is, this particular institution has been recognized as one of the top hospitals in America, earning Magnet status for nursing excellence and the highest ranking for patient, associate and physician satisfaction.

THREE KEYS OF THE THEORETICAL FRAMEWORK

IT'S A WONDERFUL THING WHEN people like Nurse Nancy find a meaningful place to work. But I would guess most of them aren't big fans of organizational theory. Still, the science of organizational behavior very much relates to Nancy's happy ending. This field of study – looking at how people function within an organizational structure to accomplish their tasks – has been ongoing for hundreds of years. While there are many theories from many authors related to organizations, three specific theories are worth referencing here: 1) cognitive dissonance theory, 2) institutional theory, and 3) sensemaking.

1. COGNITIVE DISSONANCE THEORY

The first theory is cognitive dissonance, which was created by Leon Festinger, Professor of Psychology at Stanford University. It states that an individual cannot productively function in an environment where his/her personal beliefs are inconsistent with their actions.[26] In order to get out of dissonance and into consonance, a person will either change beliefs or change behavior. Something has to give. Likewise, organizations that profess a set of core convictions but do not have consistency in behaviors will often abandon values over a period of time. Something has to give. Nurse Nancy ran into this at her third hospital. Community Heights Health professed values but aligned few behaviors to them. So naturally the staff became apathetic and cynical about the ideals proclaimed. When values aren't backed up, you will gradually lose conscientious staff and\or ultimately abandon the organization's core convictions.

2. INSTITUTIONAL THEORY

Philip Selznick, Professor Emeritus of Law and Society at the University of California, Berkeley, proposes a healthy alterative entitled "institutional theory." He defines institutional theory as organizational practices that "*infuse with value* beyond the technical requirements of the task at hand."[27] In the case of Nancy's fourth institution, Destiny Hospital, the values clearly defined there were not technically necessary to run the place, but did provide significance to the patients, associates and physicians. It's at the juncture where an organization can define what its values are and have them deeply engrained in the very culture of the institution that confessional identity is sustainable. In this framework, as Selznick writes, "organizations do not so much create values as embody them. As this occurs, the organization becomes increasingly institutionalized."[28] Therefore, "institutional survival, properly understood, is a matter of maintaining values and distinctive identity."[29]

3. SENSEMAKING

Karl Weick, a professor at the Ross School of Business at the University of Michigan, has created a body of knowledge around a simple organizational concept: individuals come into an organization, try to make sense out of various cues and clues from the environment, and then start to model their behaviors accordingly. This organizational theory is entitled Sensemaking. Regardless of what an organization states as its core values, an individual will try to understand the stimuli around them, and act accordingly.[30] That response ultimately becomes a self-fulfilling prophecy. Nurse Nancy saw this in her second job at Union Hospital. There, culture and behaviors were being driven from the associate level – regardless of the intent of the leadership team.

Let's look at these three theories – sensemaking, institutional theory, and cognitive dissonance – together. While there is no perfect theory of organizational behavior, there are insights that can be derived when the three theories are considered collectively.

An organization cannot exist over the long term if behaviors do not match beliefs. While it is admirable for leaders to state the values that they would like to *infuse* into their institution, ultimately success depends on the associates making sense of what is going around. Long-term sustainability can only occur when an organization clearly articulates its confessional identity and then infuses it into the organization in a way that causes every associate to clearly understand the core convictions (mind), practice these values in their daily behaviors (body), and gain an emotional connection with them (spirit).

THE DESTINY ZONE ASSESSMENT METHOD:
A CRITICAL QUESTION TO ASK

CENTURIES AGO, A JAPANESE GENERAL faced a formidable, well-armed opponent.   Still, even though his soldiers were greatly *outnumbered, this leader decided to attack.* What's more, the general felt confident of victory. But he understood that his men were *filled with doubt and would have to be convinced that they could prevail.* As they prepared for battle, these warriors stopped at a *religious shrine to pray for safety and victory.* After praying with the men, the general took out a coin from his pocket and said, "I shall now *toss this coin.* If it is *heads*, we shall win. If *tails*, we shall lose. Destiny will now reveal itself."

He threw the coin into the air and the entire army watched with great anticipation. As the soldiers crowded around the coin, they saw that the coin was heads. The soldiers felt a heady rush of assurance. In fact, they were so filled with *confidence* that they attacked the enemy with great zeal and emerged triumphant.

Following the victory, an astute lieutenant observed to the general, "No one can change destiny."

"Quite right," the general replied. Then he showed the lieutenant the coin. It had been stamped with heads on both sides.

By definition, destiny is something predetermined, usually an inevitable or irresistible course of events. From an organizational standpoint, the founding fathers of an institution try to create destiny by laying down a confessional identity, a collective purpose or a core ideology that they believe will be woven deeply into the fabric of an organization. Their intent is that it becomes predetermined, inevitable and irresistible. Organizational reality, however, dictates that this confessional identity can only become a predetermined destiny if it is integrated into the very nature of those who lead and function within that institution.

The fable is told of a scorpion that set out on a journey through forest and hills until he reached a river. Seeing no way to get across the water, he decided to ask a frog nearby for help. Speaking in his most polite voice, he inquired, "Would you be so kind as to give me a ride on your back across the river?"

The frog hesitated. "How do I know that if I try to help you, you won't kill me?"

"Because," the scorpion replied, "if I try to kill you, then I would die too. I cannot swim!"

Convinced by this logic, the frog allowed the scorpion to climb on his back and began swimming across the river. When they were about halfway across, the frog suddenly felt a sharp sting. Glancing up, he caught the scorpion pulling his stinger from his back. A deadening numbness began to creep into the frog's limbs.

The frog croaked, "Now we're both going to die! Why did you do that?"

The scorpion simply said, "I couldn't help myself. It is my nature."

> A critical question you must ask is: what is the nature of my organization? That is the Destiny Zone question. That is the question anyone trying to sustain a confessional identity must deal with. What is the nature of our leaders? What is the nature of our associates?

At first glance, these questions might seem somewhat ethereal, without value or concrete answers. However, the following section outlines a methodology to do precisely that. The answers can be knowable and specific. A case study within the Adventist Health System will provide an example. We'll be looking at the largest Protestant health system in America based out of Winter Park, Florida.

DISCOVERING THE NATURE OF YOUR ORGANIZATION

IF YOU HAD TO DETERMINE THE OVERALL culture or "nature" of an organization, how would you attack the assignment? And how would you impact that culture? The purpose of our proposed framework here is not to provide a step-by-step formulaic response, but rather an overall methodology that can be easily adapted and utilized in a variety of situations.

The Destiny Zone Assessment Method is outlined in Figure 2. These are the three sequential steps:

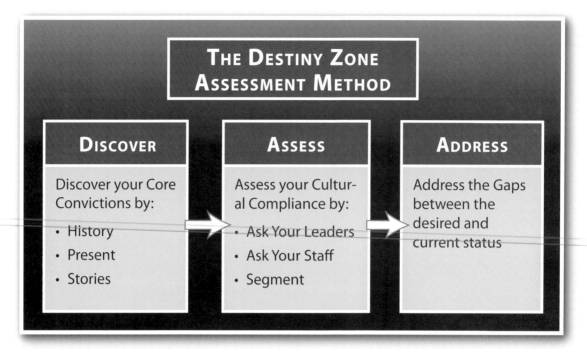

Figure 2

THE THREE-PHASE ASSESSMENT

THE TASK OF DISCOVERY is just as it sounds, a process of uncovering of what is and has been the fundamentals of the organization. This is not a process of creating something new or casting a new vision. Two researchers, Collins and Porras, picture the concept of discovery this way:

> *A very important point: You do not 'create' or 'set' core ideology. You discover core ideology. You get at it by looking inside. It has to be authentic. You can't fake an ideology. Nor can you just intellectualize it. Core values and purpose must be passionately held on a gut level, else they are not core.*[31]

1. DISCOVER

Plenty of people may wonder if they have the right skills for legitimate discovery. There's probably an excellent teacher quite near you: a two-year-old child. Find one, observe the child's interaction with the surroundings, and you will be amazed at how much can be discovered in a short time frame.

> Here's a good way to start: simply ask a lot of questions. How did this institution start? What did the founders have in mind for this organization? What philosophies did they subscribe to? What do our current leaders envision for this place? What stories do they share at orientation and during associate meetings? What does our mission statement say? What literature is available that describes the core convictions of the organization? What do associates think the core convictions are?

Once a fair amount of information has been collected during the discovery stage, the data can be grouped into themes. Those themes can be spelled out as a handful of core convictions that capture the confessional identity in a practical way. You want clear, descriptive statements of that identity.

2. ASSESS

The insightful leader is always interested in getting a picture of the culture as it actually is rather than as they assume or desire it to be. Following the discovery stage, you begin to assess. You're examining the cultural compliance of the organization. You want to determine if there is cognitive understanding, if the core convictions are being practiced on a daily basis and if there is an emotional connection to the core convictions. In essence, you're looking at the head, the hands and the heart, in order to assess wholistic adherence.

As you select people to assess, it is important to segment the participants. Look at different groups in terms of the definable roles they play in the organization. How do senior leaders compare with associates, for example? Those are key segments to assess. Several other segments you identify will depend on the organization's structure and the nature of its core convictions.

Once the groups have been segmented, a survey instrument can be developed to measure the overall adherence to the core convictions by each group. It's best if the survey can be used multiple times over a period of time so that you can assess changes or improvements in the future.

3. Address

After the survey results are evaluated, you come to the final stage: address the gaps that are identified in the assessment. The survey will help you decide the degree and nature of the intervention necessary.

ADVENTIST HEALTH SYSTEM CASE STUDY: PIONEERS IN PREVENTIVE MEDICINE

WE'LL NOW LOOK AT A CASE STUDY that illustrates this model. The Destiny Zone Assessment Method was used at Florida Hospital, located in the greater Orlando metropolitan market. Florida Hospital is not only the largest facility within the Adventist Health System, it also admits more patients for inpatient care on an annual basis than any other hospital in the United States.

From the very beginnings of the Seventh-day Adventist Church, an emphasis on health has been an integral component of its ministry and outreach. In many ways, the Seventh-day Adventist view of health is intertwined with the fundamental doctrine and practice of the church. Adventist health reformers and innovators in the nineteenth century developed a healthcare message that shaped sanitariums where individuals came to be "made well" through therapeutic treatments and to "stay well" through education. Adventists were definitely pioneers in the field of preventative medicine.

This sanitarium model has evolved, with various scientific and technological advancements, into acute care hospitals today. And those hospitals are subject to the influences and pressures that shape other medical facilities: reimbursement methods, a diverse workforce, and a healthcare model centered on disease and illness rather than health.

The original health reformation message was clearly applicable to the sanitarium model as it first developed. But in the world of the 21st century of tertiary acute-care medicine, the confessional identity of Seventh-day Adventist healthcare has become more of a challenge than a given. In taking up this challenge, understanding the original intent as compared to the current confessional identity is a critical first step. Heretofore, we haven't had much empirical data comparing current perceptions and practice within Seventh-day Adventist healthcare institutions with that original confessional identity.

> In general, Seventh-day Adventist healthcare can claim that its confessional identity has been intertwined with the church's core convictions for more than 140 years. This fact of history, however, does not guarantee that the confessional identity of yesteryear will be preserved in the future.

So the Adventist Health System case study at Florida Hospital was developed to do two things. The first purpose is to discover the confessional identity and core convictions of Seventh-day Adventist healthcare. The second objective is to evaluate the degree to which leaders and employees at the hospital align with those convictions. To gain a wholistic assessment, we will look at cognitive understanding, behaviors, and emotional attachments.

Following the Destiny Zone Assessment Method, a three-phased approach was carried out. The initial discovery phase gathered the data necessary to articulate the confessional identity and core convictions. The assessment phase determined adherence to these core convictions. Finally, the gaps which became evident were addressed.

THE DISCOVERY PHASE

IN THE DISCOVERY PHASE we included four complementary activities:

1. A historical analysis of Seventh-day Adventist healthcare through published literature

2. A survey of the official published guidelines from the General Conference of Seventh-day Adventists

3. The commission of four original "white paper" manuscripts based on current research by some of the foremost contemporary academic scholars, and

4. One-on-one interviews with 11 seasoned Adventist healthcare administrators

The following sections explain what this process revealed.

HISTORICAL ANALYSIS

As expected, a review of existing literature did produce a variety of insights regarding the original confessional identity. The Seventh-day Adventist health message emerged during the decades leading to the 20th century. In 1850, the average American life span was 39.4 years. Among newborns, 17 percent failed to reach their first birthday. Becoming a medical doctor required a mere six months of "training" and sometimes less than that. Drugs such as mercury, opium and tobacco were considered important remedies and their use was not regulated by any governmental or scientific body.[32]

Mainly through the visions and leadership of Ellen G. White, the newly formed Seventh-day Adventist church soon decided to create a formal health ministry. The early founders believed they had clear philosophical and theological reasons for doing so. The Western Health Reform Institute opened its doors in Battle Creek, Michigan on September 5, 1866 and was later renamed the Battle Creek Sanitarium.

> This institution was firmly rooted in a confessional identity, the belief that true health incorporated the whole person, including the body, mind and spirit, as demonstrated through the healing ministry of Christ. An institutionalized premise stated that every patron and employee was created in the image of God and worthy of the best care available. The Battle Creek Sanitarium provided "the combined features of a medical boarding house, hospital, religious retreat, country club, tent Chatauqua and spa."[33]

Through the capable medical directorship of Dr. John Harvey Kellogg, the Battle Creek Sanitarium became the largest of its kind in the entire world serving over 1,500 patients annually. The sanitarium also developed the reputation of being among the most scientific in the world, both in technique and equipment. A reformational zeal was definitely behind the culture at Battle Creek. The sanitarium centered its health message on eight health principles: pure air, sunlight, abstemiousness, rest, exercise, proper diet, the use of water, and trust in divine power.

GUIDELINES FROM THE SEVENTH-DAY ADVENTIST CHURCH

The church body which sponsored Battle Creek Sanitarium also provides a rich source of material. The Communications Department of the General Conference of Seventh-day Adventists has published a composite of official church positions on various topics in a publication entitled *Statements Guidelines & Other Documents*. The chapter "Health-Care Institutions" identifies ten "Operating Principles" which are summarized as follows:

1. As Christ ministered to the whole person, "the mission of the Seventh-day Adventist Church includes a ministry to the whole person – mind, body and spirit." Other aspects of Christ's ministry include "teaching the positive benefits of following the laws of health" and "the interrelationship of spiritual and natural laws."

2. As a functional and integral part of the total ministry of the church, healthcare institutions are expected to follow the standards of the church which include honoring the "sacredness of the Sabbath." Also referenced is the promotion of an "ovo-lactovegetarian diet" and abstinence from alcohol and tobacco.

3. In recognition of the dignity of man, Seventh-day Adventist healthcare institutions give high priority to personal dignity and human relationships. This manifests itself through "appropriate diagnosis, treatment by competent personnel, a caring environment, and education in healthful living."

4. A high regard for human life should be reflected in both policy and procedure.

5. Seventh-day Adventist healthcare institutions "operate as part of the community and nation in which they function" and are responsible for the health status of the community.

6. Clergy of all creeds are welcome to visit with their parishioners.

7. The mission of Seventh-day Adventist healthcare is carried out through compassionate, competent staff that delivers care in accordance with the practices and standards of the Church.

8. Each institution is to operate in a financially responsible manner.

9. Primary prevention and health education are to be an integral part of the healthcare institution.

10. Seventh-day Adventist healthcare institutions are to function in consultation with the Health and Temperance Department of the General Conference of Seventh-day Adventists.

WHITE PAPER MANUSCRIPTS

Now we moved to the next component of our discovery phase about the confessional identity of Seventh-day Adventist healthcare. It was something that complements the historical literature. We commissioned four original white paper manuscripts based on current research by some of the foremost contemporary scholars of the Seventh-day Adventist Church. These papers were authored by Dr. Fritz Guy of La Sierra University, Dr. Richard Rice of Loma Linda University, Dr. Alden Thompson of Walla Walla University, and Dr. Harold Koenig of Duke University. After completion, the papers were presented to the senior leadership of Florida Hospital at a retreat at Celebration Health, Florida.

At the conclusion of the retreat, both the authors and the hospital leadership joined in an exercise to synthesize a confessional identity based on the white papers and the professional experience of the participants. This is what they determined:

1. The Seventh-day Adventist view of "Health & Healing" begins with a perspective on what it means to be human. The collective belief is that being human means being a whole person, inclusive of mind, body and soul as one reality.

2. Another perspective of being human is that we are created in the image of God. This reality creates a moral imperative that Seventh-day Adventist healthcare will be inspired to serve all mankind as a spiritual calling.

3. Health and healing are two sides of the same coin.

4. A whole-person care approach cares for people physically, spiritually, socially and emotionally.

5. To pursue whole-person care requires a wholistic organization. Healing requires the whole person.

6. With the significance of its size and influence, Florida Hospital can and should impact healthcare policy.

7. Seventh-day Adventists hold polarities in balance, recognizing truth within the paradox of episodic care vs. community care, caring for a patient vs. caring with, healing vs. health, stability vs. investment, and business vs. ministry.

8. As we deal with change in the 21ˢᵗ century, "Love to God & Love to Man" is the bedrock construct for Seventh-day Adventist healthcare.

9. Sin does not separate, it distorts.

INTERVIEWS

The final component of our discovery phase involved personal interviews. We talked with eleven seasoned Seventh-day Adventist healthcare administrators chosen for their unique experiences and professional backgrounds. On average, these administrators have more than thirty years of service in Seventh-day Adventist healthcare. Through a structured interview process, four questions were provided prior to the meeting, and the dialogue was recorded, transcribed and analyzed. We focused on eight themes referenced by the majority of the participants. What we found is whereas the previous discovery methods did provide good information and straightforward insights, it was really these interviews that fleshed out the discovery.

When asked to identify the confessional identity of Seventh-day Adventist healthcare, every administrator interviewed referenced wholeness. Their comments included:

- "Seventh-day Adventists have a very unique way of treating an individual from not only the physical aspects but their mind and spirit as well."

- "We uniquely believe in an intersecting mind, body, spirit model that has the three rings intersect in a way that there is influence across the three."

- "Wholeness is philosophically and theologically the absolute most authentic base to minister because it is biblical – it is the biblical model of who people are."

Ten individuals referenced the healing ministry of Christ specifically, when talking about confessional identity. Specific statements are as follows:

- "Seventh-day Adventist hospitals should model our lives and the work of our institutions after the life and work of Jesus Christ."

- "This is a Christian organization where Christian values are lived every day and it is affecting the way that we provide care."

- "Simply stated, we extend the healing ministry of Christ."

Ten individuals also made reference to certain health principles originally identified by Ellen G. White: pure air, sunlight, abstemiousness, rest, exercise, proper diet, the use of water and trust in divine power. Florida Hospital has developed a contemporary adaptation of those principles entitled CREATION Health. That acronym stands for Choice, Rest, Environment, Activity, Trust in divine power, Interpersonal relationships, Outlook and Nutrition.

As identified by nine individuals, one of the essential tenets of the Seventh-day Adventist faith is the seventh-day Sabbath as a day of rest, a day to connect with God. They spoke of the health benefits associated with a weekly Sabbath rest. They also stated that this special day should be a blessing for all those within a Seventh-day Adventist hospital, including patients, physicians and associates.

Seven of those interviewed highlighted the importance of a Seventh-day Adventist hospital to the health status of the community. The same number spoke of the importance of having Seventh-day Adventist leadership in key positions within every Seventh-day Adventist hospital. Six individuals expressed the belief that people being created in the "Image of God" is a fundamental understanding that undergirds the confessional identity of Seventh-day Adventist healthcare. Six of those interviewed also stated that the overall environment and "spirit of service" should be so pervasive as to be "palpably Christian," one "where Seventh-day Adventism is proudly displayed."

DISCOVERY OF THE CONFESSIONAL IDENTITY

In the end, the process of discovery gave us a compelling and clear picture of the confessional identity of Seventh-day Adventist healthcare. Based on this broad base of input and perspective, it ultimately includes:

- Wholeness

- The Healing Ministry of Christ

- Health Principles

- Honoring the Beliefs of the Seventh-day Adventist Church

- Recognizing Every Person as a Creation Formed in the Image of God

- Service to the Community

Considering the input from all sources queried, the core convictions are described as follows:

Wholeness – Wholeness is the integration of the mind and body with the spirit, giving people the ability to experience the fullness of life. According to this view, the physical aspects of medicine are only one component of true health. Every part of a person, including emotional state, social well-being, and spiritual condition, needs to be considered and addressed. In other words, all the dimensions of a human being are interconnected and cannot be separated.

The Healing Ministry of Christ – During His life on earth, Jesus Christ spent the majority of time teaching and healing people, dealing with the physical and spiritual needs of those He came in contact with. That's how He carried out His mission of bringing us restoration to our heavenly Father. That ministry of Christ should be prevalent in word, symbol, and practice within a Seventh-day Adventist healthcare institution. Practical applications would include teaching, prayer, spiritual nurturing, care, and compassion which are motivated by the loving example of Jesus Christ.

Seventh-day Adventist Beliefs – As a ministry of the Seventh-day Adventist Church, health clinics and hospitals such as Florida Hospital are extensions of the belief system determined by the church. In addition to extending loving and compassionate care as demonstrated by Jesus Christ, being faithful to all biblical teachings, including honoring Saturday as the Sabbath, is core to the Seventh-day Adventist belief system.

Image of God – As reflected in the biblical book of Genesis, man and woman were created in the image of God. This means that all individuals are of great value regardless of their race, gender, or social status. Therefore, all people should be afforded the highest levels of dignity.

Community – Seventh-day Adventist healthcare institutions were established as part of a reformation message in the 1860s as a community service that promoted health, wholeness, and ultimate restoration. Therefore, it is imperative that the betterment of the community health status be of significant ongoing concern. In addition to services provided within hospitals and health institutions, extended activities such as community clinics and events such as blood drives, heart walks and health screenings are of core significance.

THE ASSESSMENT PHASE

A T THIS JUNCTURE, WE HAVE COMPLETED our first task – to identify the core convictions. Now we are ready to move on to the second phase – to assess how the organization aligns and adheres to the core convictions. To fully assess the cultural compliance of the organization, it is essential to determine if:

1. There is cognitive understanding

2. The core convictions are being practiced on a daily basis, and

3. There is an emotional connection to the core convictions

In essence, this wholistic adherence assesses the head, the hands and the heart.

In assessing the organization, it is important to segment the participants into a variety of cohorts so that one can determine the level of adherence at each level of the organization. These include the senior leaders, middle management and the associates. The other segments will depend on the organization and nature of the confessional identity and core convictions.

For the purposes of this case study, demographic information was collected to allow the data to be segmented by years of service with Florida Hospital and by religious affiliation.

For this case study, the questions to be assessed are as follows:

1. To what degree and in what ways are the current leaders and associates' perceptions at Florida Hospital aligned with the identified core convictions?

2. To what degree and in what ways do the senior leaders, middle management, and associates understand, behave and emotionally connect with these core convictions?

3. To what degree and in what ways do the associates within religious groups align with the core convictions?

4. To what degree and in what ways do the associates within religious groups understand, behave and emotionally connect with these core convictions?

The assessment included a total of 653 associates of Florida Hospital who were asked to complete a 44-question survey. It was scored on a 5-point Likert scale that was formatted around the six core convictions. The survey population was divided into three groups: senior leaders ($n - 41$), middle management ($n - 215$), and associates ($n - 397$). In assessing the responses among these three segmented populations, various statistical methods were used to quantify variances. We wanted to zero in on precisely where alignments existed and where statistically significant gaps were present.

The specific results of the questionnaire are formatted around four questions which we want to test.

QUESTION ONE: Alignment by Organizational Level

The first question to be assessed asks: "To what degree and in what ways are the current leaders and associate perceptions at Florida Hospital aligned with the identified core convictions?" Here is what we found as featured in Figure 3. Based on the 5-point scale, the average across all five questions was roughly 4.1 which would indicate a solid alignment overall. In assessing by individual core conviction, the highest adherence was with the Healing Ministry of Christ and the lowest was with Wholeness. Currently, there is no established standard to determine what level of adherence constitutes alignment consistent with the Destiny Zone. However, these levels would suggest a relatively high adherence.

However, it is not sufficient to only assess based on overall scores – for the sake of determining the organizational ability to live within a status of cognitive consonance, it is important to drill down to the next level to determine if any gaps exist between the senior leaders, middle management and associates.

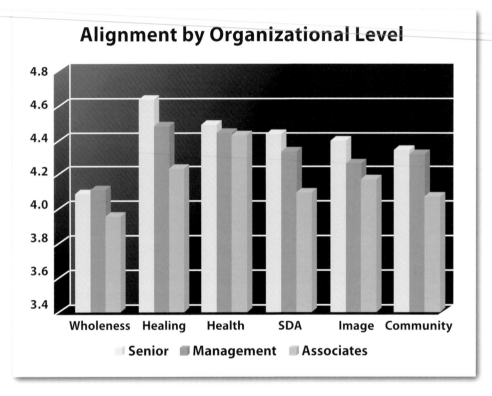

Figure 3

The three groups scored very similarly when it came to the six core convictions (although different responses to the Healing Ministry of Christ approached statistical significance). The picture was a little different when it came to comparing associates with senior leaders. Statistically significant differences appeared in responses to questions about four out of the six core convictions (Healing Ministry, Honor Seventh-day Adventist Beliefs, Image of God, and Community).

There were also differences between middle management and associates. Statistically significant variations appeared in statements about the following four (out of six) core convictions: Wholeness, Healing Ministry of Christ, Honor Seventh-day Adventist Beliefs, and Community.

Interestingly enough, there was one area in which full alignment was determined across all three segmented groups. That was the area of Health Principles.

IMPLICATIONS

The overall scores across the survey would suggest a fairly strong adherence to the core convictions. Granted, there are some levels of difference between core convictions like Health Principles compared to Wholeness. Yet, with an overall score of over 4.1 on average, there appears to be a healthy organizational understanding and commitment to the core convictions.

However, the survey data spotlights something to be concerned about. There's a gap between the big picture (the value system of institutional theory) and daily life in an institution (the sensemaking factor where people put theory into practice). That gap indicates dissonance that needs to be bridged so that daily life is more consistent with the big picture. Over the longer term, it will likely prove problematic to have the gap between the leadership team (senior leaders and middle management) and associates. As noted in the confessional identity matrix, when there are clearly articulated core convictions without employee adherence – confessional identity is potentially at-risk. The data in this assessment would indicate that Florida Hospital functions within the Destiny Zone. Having said that, it will be essential to intentionally advance the core convictions with associates to ensure that Florida Hospital stays in the Destiny Zone.

There is a very practical and organizational view that needs to be considered here.

For some organizations, the idea to *infuse value* beyond what is absolutely necessary to complete a task required takes time, energy and resources. In view of the financial and operational constraints on the healthcare industry today, it's increasingly difficult to promote practices that are perceived as inefficient or irrelevant. This could make institutional values secondary to the mandates of an external agency.

Let's consider the following practical example. A surgery today cannot begin without staff members completing the national patient safety guideline checklist. On the other hand, something like ensuring a wholistic approach to patient care might be considered optional. Any surgery will be stopped if the "site and side" policy has not been completed. But what if a patient would like a prayer offered before the procedure? Would people be willing to delay an operation for that reason? Some who oversee healthcare in general might discount a time of prayer in the operating room as automatically inefficient. But that's one practice that definitely reflects and sustains institutional core convictions. A confessional identity is diluted if the spiritual side of healing is de-emphasized. Do we really want to preserve core convictions? Then the practice of wholistic care and prayer has to be elevated to the same level of importance as external regulatory mandates.

QUESTION TWO: Wholistic Adherence

Our second question asks: "To what degree and in what ways do the senior leaders, middle management, and associates cognitively understand, behave and emotionally connect with these core convictions?" In other words, we want to look at mind, body and heart – across the three teams. We formulated specific questions in the survey that addressed these facets of core convictions.

The results? As noted in Figure 4, across all three groups there was a clear cognitive understanding of the core convictions. In fact, on a five-point scale, all three groups indicate a strong understanding of the core convictions, with all groups scoring higher than 4.5, on average. This is a very impressive and positive finding!

It is quite noteworthy to see that despite strong cognitive understanding, there are much lower scores on the behavioral component. How concerning is this? To a significant degree this is to be expected as part of our human condition. Let me use two examples to illustrate this point.

- Many of us know that we should exercise daily but most of us fail to do so.

- Likewise, nearly everyone knows that we should eat five to six servings of fruits and vegetables each day – but many times that simply does not happen with everyone.

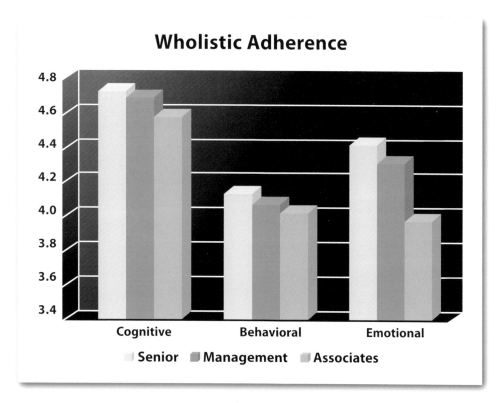

Figure 4

So again we ask – how concerning is this? The answer is one of judgment to assess an acceptable level of dissonance between knowing and doing. In this case, the difference seems to be large enough to warrant concern.

One mitigating factor to resolve this dissonance is for the emotional aspect to reconcile the cognitive and behavioral. The formula is well tested in research and is fairly simple to follow. If you want to change behavior, tap into the emotional aspect in order to achieve lasting change. The fact that the scores on the emotional component are generally around 4.0, there seems to be an adequate emotional quotient to convict the behavioral change necessary to be more aligned with the cognitive understanding.

Another area to examine is between the senior leaders, middle management and associates. Full alignment across all three segmented groups appeared in only one component: the behavioral. When looking at all three components: cognitive, behavioral and emotional, full alignment appeared only between two of the groups:

senior leaders and middle management. And again, statistically significant differences showed up between senior leaders and the associates – especially when it came to cognitive understanding and emotional connection.

The same held true when comparing the responses of middle management with those of associates. Statistically significant differences showed up between those two groups in the areas of cognitive understanding and emotional connection. In fact, the most statistically significant differences always appeared between associates and leadership – both senior leaders and middle management.

IMPLICATIONS

One of the propositions behind the research is this: current actions must align with stated core convictions if an organization is to preserve its confessional identity. Misalignments or gaps produce disconnects. A healthy identity requires alignment. Current practice needs to fit core convictions. Our data suggest there are gaps between the leadership team and the associates, different levels of cognitive understanding, behavioral adherence, and emotional connection.

The data also reveals a gap between cognitive understanding and behavioral adherence in each of the three levels within Florida Hospital. Behavioral mean scores were significantly lower than cognitive scores – across all three segmented populations. In other words, what the mind comprehends is disconnected to some degree from what the hand is doing and what the heart holds dear. Christine Oliver of York University, Toronto, notes in her work on the antecedents to deinstitutionalization that under certain specific conditions, institutional values and traditions are "vulnerable to challenge, reassessment or rejection."[34] In particular, if an institutional value is "no longer reproduced or reenacted over time,"[35] it may well be set aside as irrelevant. That's precisely the peril a low behavioral mean score points out.

This is the junction where institutional theory and sensemaking must come together – where institutional theory is the construct, sensemaking is the process. For that construct to remain intact, the process must support it. Actions have to fit principles. Behaviors have to fit core convictions. The day-to-day actions need to flesh out the big picture.

That's the challenge at Florida Hospital that our data highlights.

These results raise a number of daunting questions: Why is there a gap between the cognitive and behavioral scores across all levels in the organization? What factors are leading to the gulf between the leadership team and the associates? Is there a gap in communication between the leadership team and the associates? Are the associates simply reflecting the behaviors they perceive to be of greatest significance to the leadership team?

After reflecting on these questions, I am convinced that the sustenance of the Seventh-day Adventist health core convictions depends on this one crucial issue: focusing on behaviors and emotional commitment across all levels within the organization. That's the only way values will be internalized, the only way they'll be reproduced from one generation to the next. To really last, they have to be organizationally embedded.

QUESTION THREE: Alignment by Faith Group

The third question inquires: "To what degree and in what ways do the associates within religious groups align with the core convictions?" To test this, we looked at Florida Hospital staff members who came from a variety of religious backgrounds. What we discovered as shown in Figure 5 was this: full alignment in the areas of the Healing Ministry and Community. In other words, people of various faiths ascribed to similar values related to Healing Ministry and Community.

The other four core convictions scored a bit differently. Full alignment came out most clearly among people who identified with Christian-based religions (Protestant, Roman Catholic, Seventh-day Adventist) for all of the core convictions. It was also determined that no statistically significant difference existed between the Christian-based religions and the Other Religions. Statistically significant differences did show up, however, when we compared the responses of people with a religious affiliation with those who claimed "No Religion."

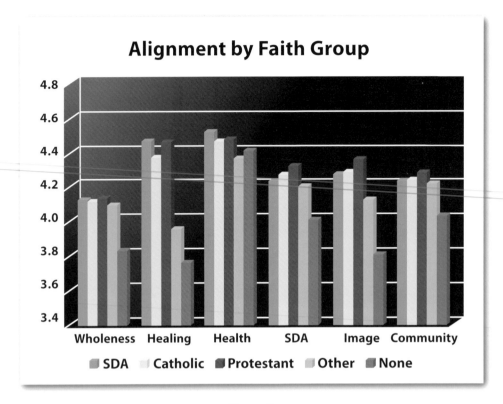

Figure 5

This is a remarkable finding. Of those with a stated faith background, there were very few statistical differences across the six core convictions. The only group that had lower scores was those with no religious affiliation. Let's now look at the wholistic adherence to see if there are similar findings.

QUESTION FOUR: Wholistic Adherence by Faith Group

Our fourth question is closely tied to the third. The question reads: "To what degree and in what ways do the associates within religious groups cognitively understand, behave and emotionally connect with these core convictions?" Now we were looking more closely at how the hand and heart, as well as the mind, align with the confessional identity based on faith affiliation. As noted in Figure 6, there were very high and similar scores that existed amongst those professing a faith affiliation.

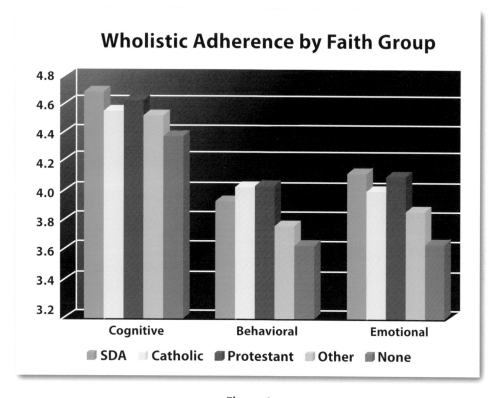

Figure 6

In terms of differences, what our survey showed were that differences at these levels did exist. The most significant statistical difference appeared again when we compared those having a Christian-based religion with those who indicated "None" for religious affiliation.

So again, yes, the head, hand and heart were aligned with core convictions among people with a Christian faith; less so among people without a religious identification.

IMPLICATIONS

In sharing these results, the findings by faith group have raised a significant amount of interest and discussion. In essence, for those individuals who identify themselves with a Christian faith group, there is a similarity in understanding, behavior and emotional connection across the six core convictions. Where much is made regarding the difference between various religions, there seems to be a unifying theme in extending the healing ministry of Christ.

While the healing ministry of Christ is an area that can easily be understood from a broad Christian perspective, what about the areas that are more particular and unique to the Seventh-day Adventist belief system? According to the survey, responses to the core conviction entitled "Honoring the Beliefs of the Seventh-day Adventist Church," the scores were very similar amongst the Christian-based faith groups. Despite the fact that many of these individuals do not profess the particular beliefs of the Seventh-day Adventist Church, there is a sacred bond of faith that seems to be prevalent at Florida Hospital.

Let me share a recent example to illustrate. One of the sacred beliefs of the Seventh-day Adventist Church is the practice to honor and connect with God and our fellow man through a special Sabbath celebration from sundown Friday through Saturday. This belief was tested in a very practical way. In order to pour the concrete foundation for a new patient tower on the Orlando campus, the general contractor specified the absolute necessity to start the 36 hour process Friday night during Sabbath hours. The decision was made to accept the risks associated with deferring the pour until the after Sabbath on Saturday night. In anticipation of the pour, associates across Florida Hospital prayed and expressed pride that Florida Hospital chose to be faithful to its core convictions. Even though many of these associates are not Seventh-day Adventists, they understood the importance, supported the decision and were further emotionally connected to Florida Hospital honoring the Sabbath.

Stories like this demonstrate an organizational maturity in relation to its confessional identity. In this case, the commonality of faith seems to be a unifying factor that can be a driving force in sustaining the confessional identity.

Through this survey and analysis, it is evident that the key components necessary to sustain confessional identity are modeled around a "head, hand and heart" approach. In other words, the entire organization must have a deep understanding of the confessional identity (head), behave accordingly (hand), and be inspired by a deep passion (heart) for those items that the organization has defined as the essential core.

In reflection of the four questions explored in this survey, we are reminded that there is some organizational disconnect between the leadership and associates on many of the core convictions. There is also the concerning difference between what is cognitively known compared to what is practiced. Cognitive Dissonance Theory reminds us that individuals cannot remain in a divided world where a belief is professed but not practiced. Given the survey results, there is additional focus that is necessary at Florida Hospital to bring complete consonance. How is this accomplished? What steps can an organization take to bring behavioral consistency? How can leadership create an organization that is deeply committed to sustaining core convictions? These questions are addressed in the following section.

EXPERIENCING CONFESSIONAL IDENTITY: HOW TO CREATE DEEPLY COMMITED STAKEHOLDERS

A N ORGANIZATION IS NEVER MORE THAN one generation away from losing its confessional identity. This statement unsettles me to my core, but at the same time, motivates me to ensure that the decisions that I am a part of and the people that are being developed around me are intentionally groomed to understand, practice and have an emotional attachment to the organization's confessional identity.

So we return to the questions posed in the previous section. What steps can an organization take to bring behavioral consistency? How can leadership create an organization that is deeply committed to sustain their core convictions?

The answers can be found in the *"Head, Hand and Heart"* approach. While many times we think of organizations in terms of their marble headquarters, manufacturing plants and corporate logos, the reality is they are a collection of individuals harnessed together by a common collective purpose. Each of these individuals has a head, two hands and a heart that ultimately determine organizational direction.

The importance of this model is the connection back to the Destiny Zone. As demonstrated by the graphic in Figure 7, it is in the "sweet spot" between the three interlocking circles of

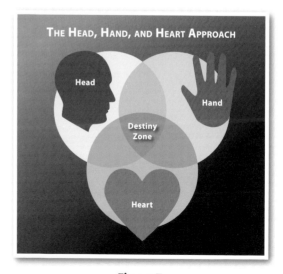

Figure 7

the head, hand and heart that an organization can fulfill its destiny. An organization can ensure that the confessional identity is fully aligned towards the organization's purpose when the entire organization is wholistically engaged. The "head" has a clear understanding of the organization's confessional identity. The "hand" is consistently bringing the confessional identity to life by behaviors and actions. The "heart" brings a zeal and sense of meaning to the cause.

In considering these three components, the following are practical steps that any leader can immediately pursue with the *Head, Hand and Heart* approach. While there are hundreds of practical activities and tactics that could be utilized in the *Head, Hand and Heart* approach, the following ideas are a sampling to inspire your thinking.

MAKING IT PRACTICAL

1. **Stimulate the *Head* by:**

   - **Clarifying Your Confessional Identity** – Developing a clear and concise articulation of your confessional identity for your Board, leaders and associates to have and understand.

   - **Offering Educational Retreats** – Building the case for your confessional identity through educational retreats where leaders can step away from work place pressures and focus on the organization's core convictions.

   - **Planning Broad Communication** – Articulating and educating on your confessional identity through printed materials and seminars.

   - **Integrating Into New Employee Orientation** – Dedicating significant time and effort in new associate orientation and ongoing educational sessions to understanding the meaning and purpose of the organization.

2. **Commission the *Hand* by:**

   - **Encouraging Experiential Learning** – Fostering experiential learning opportunities through simulated scenarios.

Commissioning Leadership From All Levels – Select champions who will bring the front-line perspective. Appoint these associates as your ambassadors of the confessional identity.

Incorporating Confessional Identity Into Annual Reviews – Including the confessional identity behaviors in the annual reviews of your leaders and associates gives it added credibility.

Evaluating Daily Behaviors – Hiring secret shoppers to witness and evaluate daily behaviors.

3. **Engage the *Heart* by:**

Using Stories – Stories have the incredible ability to stimulate an emotional connection and bring a different level of attachment to a cause. These stories should demonstrate the power that happens when the confessional identity is practiced. Within the healthcare field, highlighting "Mission Moments" when associates embodied the mission, or highlight a patient experience that exemplifies the power of the confessional identity.

Renewing Passion for the Profession – Centering the associate back to the reason they chose to pursue the profession and the passion that resides within each human being to serve and make a difference.

Focusing on Significance – Recasting "the job" into "a calling" of higher purpose and significance.

Considering the Use of Commitment Exercises – Commitment exercises such as retreats, pledge forms and re-enactments of historical or desired events.

Drawing on Existing Insight – Tapping into the experience and insight of your Board, former leaders and colleagues in the industry.

This is the sweet spot that every organization should seek to find. This is where the true confessed identity of an organization is understood, practiced and appreciated. This is where destiny happens.

A PERSONAL STORY OF EXPERIENCING CONFESSIONAL IDENTITY IN ACTION

TO ILLUSTRATE THE CONCEPTS EXPLORED in the Adventist Health System Case Study, the following story exemplifies how the confessional identity is experienced in a real and practical way. This story is more than theoretical, it is personal. This story is used in closing to demonstrate the importance and impact that occurs when an organization fully embraces its sacred purpose and puts flesh to the concept in a spirit of loving service.

> My study of Seventh-day Adventist healthcare is more than an academic interest to me. It's personal. It has grown into a passion. During my 20 years of working in a variety of capacities at Florida Hospital and Porter Adventist Hospital, I have, on several occasions been moved to tears by letters from patients and their families. These are letters of appreciation for a hospital stay that can best be described as a sacred experience.

But this passion of mine is also based on more than the experiences of former patients. It's based on more than my vocation. It started with something that happened to me personally.

Before the birth of our first child, my wife Cindy and I did everything most expectant parents do. We joyfully prepared the baby's crib and room. We made many trips to Babies-R-Us. We digested every page of the book, "What to Expect When Your Expecting." Everything revolved around the prospect of adding seven pounds of elation to our lives.

Through the wonders of ultrasound, we got a fuzzy picture of our child, discovering that God would bless us with a daughter. Instantaneously, pink became our favorite color. "Barbie" became a best friend. Yes we were naïve in our anticipation. Yes we were rookies in this whole parenting enterprise. But the love affair had already begun. We couldn't stop longing for that miraculous day when this little girl would be placed in our arms.

That day actually came sooner than either of us planned. One Saturday night in mid-summer, while Cindy and I were at home watching a movie, she placed my hand on her tummy to feel the baby moving around in her womb. The fetal activity felt different, more vigorous than the usual baby's limb pushing here or there. Maybe more like a contraction. But we dismissed the thought. Ten minutes later it happened again. Yes it did feel like a contraction. And another five minutes later. Then three minutes.

Hurrying into our car with Cindy, I did my best impression of an ambulance driver – without the benefit of lights or siren – as we raced to Florida Hospital. We made it safely and the obstetrician confirmed that Cindy was indeed in pre-term labor. She was almost three months early, at only 27 weeks gestation. Fortunately medication stabilized the situation and the contractions stopped.

With the crisis averted, the clinical staff began to focus on the why. What had caused this pre-term labor? Florida Hospital had recently recruited a perinatologist with an obstetrical subspecialty who restricts his practice to the care of the mother and fetus in high risk pregnancy situations just like ours. After scanning our baby with ultrasound, the physician began to study the baby's stomach. At that point it was an area smaller than the fingernail on my pinky finger. Even so, the perinatologist made a firm diagnosis: duodenal atresia. That's a clinical term for a very frightening situation wherein the first part of the small intestine is totally blocked. Since the fetus is unable to process or digest the amniotic fluid, pressure accumulates on the mother's cervix sending her into pre-term labor.

For the next ten weeks, Cindy was confined to bed rest except for the weekly trips to the perinatologist. He was trying to determine at precisely what point the high-powered medication necessary to maintain the pregnancy might start damaging the baby's heart. From time to time, using a ten-inch needle, he also performed an amniocentesis to determine if our baby's lungs were developed enough to be viable. My wife and I felt terribly grateful for the medical technologies that allow a physician to diagnose an issue the size of your fingernail in utero, and then have the pharmaceutical ability to stave off a pending delivery because lab tests showed the lungs are not yet developed. Amazing!

Thankfully, the care plan at Florida Hospital succeeded and our baby was able to remain in the womb for 37 weeks. Still, so much amniotic fluid had accumulated inside

Cindy during this time that we could only imagine our daughter must be developing into an excellent swimmer! A birth date had to be set before the pressure built to the point of possibly bursting Cindy's uterus. But the drama was just beginning.

When the appointed day came, the staff in the delivery room had to prepare for the gallons of amniotic fluid that would be released at birth. But aside from that, everyone expected a normal and uneventful delivery. Cindy went into labor. The contractions intensified. The stage was set for the long awaited birth. But then the fetal monitoring equipment began sending warning signals. We stared at the signs of our baby's distress in horror. The concern was obvious on the obstetrician's face.

And it was all happening with our daughter already in the birth canal. She'd become stuck there. It was too late for delivery by caesarian section. Somehow they had to get this baby out as soon as possible. Minutes passed. I prayed desperately as the obstetrician tried every technique in the book to dislodge our daughter. I could see the agony on Cindy's face.

Then finally, after what seemed like hours, our daughter made her appearance into the world. Cindy and I waited breathlessly for the baby's first cry. Our hearts pounded in our chests as we looked for some sign of the baby's pulse.

But she was ashen and limp. We'd already given her a name, Bailey. But Cindy couldn't hold our firstborn in her arms. The staff whisked our daughter away immediately to the neonatal team. They began their work with great clinical precision and expertise.

Every newborn is evaluated on an Apgar Scale that quantifies an infant's overall health on a scale from one to ten. Heart rate, skin complexion, respiration, reflexes and muscle tone are all assessed. Normal healthy babies score in a range of seven to ten. Bailey scored a one. After ten minutes, the neonatal team managed to get her up to a three – while an improvement, our baby was still in a very dire state. While her heart was beating, other systems were not functioning properly.

I still vividly remember sitting with the neonatologist, Dr. Eduardo Lugo, as he explained the severity of the situation. He described in detail that our daughter had very little blood volume in her body. Although not diagnosed, the likelihood was a bleed in the brain. It was heartbreaking news. And yet I could still sense the caring and the empathy in his voice. Dr. Lugo had to tell us that it was unlikely Bailey would make it through the night. And even if she did, she had little chance of becoming a normal healthy child. And yet he didn't deliver this as simply scientific information. There was a real human being there, talking to another human being who was dangling on the edge of fatherhood.

At this point Cindy and I understood all too clearly that even the latest in medical technology has its limits. But there was still something else we could cling to as a lifeline. And that was our faith, a belief that a God who gave up His Son is there with us in the worst of times, and that He isn't above doing miracles sometimes. That's where we experienced a real difference at Florida Hospital.

Many other medical facilities could have provided the equipment, the technology and the physician skills to care for our daughter. But they could not have provided something else. As the physicians and nurses swarmed around our daughter, providing state-of-the-art critical care medicine, a separate group of caregivers and chaplains focused their love and attention on Cindy and me. They spoke with us at appropriate times. They prayed with us. They helped us get in touch with the love and strength that only God can provide in situations like these. These people didn't promise a miracle. In fact, they prepared us for the possibility that our dream of a healthy, perfect daughter might not come true. But what they did do was help create an atmosphere of trust. They helped us affirm the fact that we are a valuable part of God's family – whatever might happen in this moment of crisis. Through it all, they created something I can only call the "spirit" of medicine.

It was that delivery room experience that has helped me understand much more deeply that faith is indeed a critical component of healthcare. It provides a spirit of hope and support that even the best of medical science can never create. And it's only within faith-based facilities like Florida Hospital that these more wholistic options are offered. During that long night I was keenly aware of a confessional identity being understood, practiced, and emotionally real. I knew this experience could be reproduced in few other places. And that's the fundamental reason I am passionate about Seventh-day Adventist healthcare.

In sharing my experience with many different groups over the years, I often have not revealed the end of the story. That's because I want the focus to be on the spirit of Seventh-day Adventist healthcare – regardless of any particular outcome. And I'm well aware of many families who have endured a tragic loss in similar situations. Just a year before the birth of our daughter, Cindy and I grieved with dear friends who had suffered through the delivery of a stillborn baby.

But people still always ask me how things turned out. They want to know. Well, we were very blessed. The truth is, our daughter made it through that horrible night. The staff at Florida Hospital helped our little girl every perilous step of the way. The blood volumes were restored to normal. Through surgical intervention, the intestinal blockage issue was resolved. Yes, the word "miracle" does pop up when Cindy and I talk about it.

Today Bailey is a healthy and happy 14-year-old, who fully enjoys her friends and excels in academics at Mile High Academy. Like most parents, we can't begin to count the ways in which this little girl has brought joy into our lives. And that joy is multiplied immeasurably when we reflect back on the night of her birth when God carried us through agonizing hours, with the help of loving, supportive staff members at Florida Hospital. So I will always be inspired to bring the spirit of faith to those that we care for in our hospitals.

SOMETHING WORTH HOLDING ON TO

ULTIMATELY, A CONFESSIONAL identity is very personal. Yes, a confessional identity is institutional. But in the end, it is personal. It was personal for Mabel, the woman who wrote me the letter stating, "Every day and every experience was a reflection of your mission statement." This daily alignment between intent and daily occurrence is what every organization should aspire to. In the case of Adventist Health System, the organizational purpose is to create a destiny of extending the healing ministry of Christ. My wife and I experienced this organizational purpose in a very real and personal way with the birth of our daughter Bailey.

It is for these reasons that we must protect our confessional identity. Creating and sustaining a confessional identity is a sacred calling that is worth holding on to.

FLORIDA HOSPITAL
HEALTHCARE
& LEADERSHIP
MONOGRAPH SERIES

We would like to hear from you.
Please send your comments about this monograph
to us in care of Comments@FLHosp.org. Thank you.

ACKNOWLEDGEMENTS

THIS MONOGRAPH REFLECTS A PASSION that has motivated me for over twenty years. This passion to preserve the integrity of Seventh-day Adventist healthcare has matured through the years and will certainly continue to be my lifelong ambition. This topic has not only served as the subject matter for my doctoral dissertation, but is the reason that I am excited to start my day at Porter Adventist Hospital each morning.

Through the years, I have been mentored and inspired by great leaders within the Adventist Health System and Florida Hospital like Mardian Blair, Tom Werner, Don Jernigan, Rich Reiner, Lars Houmann and Terry Shaw. In an attempt to discover our confessional identity and instill these core convictions into daily practice, the journey has been deeply enriched by my colleagues at Florida Hospital including Des Cummings, Ted Hamilton, Brian Paradis, David Banks, Terry Owen, Dick Tibbits, Bill Wilson, Connie Hamilton, Beth Weagraff, Monica Reed and many others.

From an academic perspective, Shirley Freed skillfully guided my path through the dissertation process. Duane Covrig provided incredible organizational theory insight and Sy Saliba served as a faithful counselor throughout the process. I'm also grateful to a number of professionals who provided invaluable feedback on the manuscript as it was being shaped including: Stephen King, Jim Feldbush, Rick Stiffney, Chris Thomason, Mike Toupin, and Peter Bath.

A special note of appreciation is owed to Todd Chobotar who relentlessly encouraged the development of this monograph. In his role as Director of Publishing at Florida Hospital, Todd has pursued the development of this text for over three years. Thank you Todd for your persistence. My thanks also to Stephanie Rick and Lillian Boyd on the Publishing team who provided coordination of resources and support that took this project across the finish line. And many thanks to Steven Mosely whose skill and encouragement helped take an academic dissertation and transform it into the monograph it is today.

Of greatest significance, a special note of gratitude to my wife Cindy and our three daughters Bailey, Kennedy and Hadley. Thank you for your love and support that allows me to pursue my passion. Each of you brings meaning to my life and essence to my soul.

It is my prayer that the Lord God be glorified and that the healing ministry of Christ will be extended through this sacred work.

APPENDIX:

CONFESSIONAL IDENTITY QUESTIONNAIRE – A SURVEY ON INSTITUTIONAL VALUES

Purpose: The purpose of this questionnaire is to determine the gaps and alignments between the institutional values of Seventh-day Adventist healthcare and the understanding, behaviors, and emotions of employees at Florida Hospital in Orlando, Florida.

To accurately assess the current beliefs, behaviors and feelings by the employees of Florida Hospital, it is critical that you respond to this survey. Please answer the questions exactly as you perceive them and not according t how you believe the organization or any individual may wish for you to reply. Your honest assessment will help Florida Hospital determine the levels of understanding and engagement on the six institutional values as defined below.

Participation Agreement: As this is an online survey, completing and returning the survey will constitute your consent to participate in this research study. Your participation is voluntary and individual confidentiality will be assured in the analysis and reporting of all data. There are no known risks for participation in this study. To review the complete research protocol and informed consent form, please visit here: www.flhosp.org/database/protocol

Directions: The following rating scale should be used to evaluate the six institutional values of Florida Hospital. After reviewing the definitions for each of the institutional values, circle the rating that best applies based on your assessment and understanding of Florida Hospital. This survey should take approximately 10 minutes to complete.

1. Strongly Disagree
2. Disagree
3. Undecided
4. Agree
5. Strongly Agree
N/A   Unknown

Thank you for your participation.

I. WHOLENESS – The integration of the mind and body with the spirit to enjoy the fullness of life. According to this view, the physical aspects of medicine are only one component of true health. For a full life, all aspects of a person including their emotional status, social, and spiritual health need to be considered and addressed. In other words, all aspects of a person are interconnected and cannot be separated.

1.	I understand Florida Hospital's concept of wholeness.	1	2	3	4	5	N/A
2.	I believe in the importance of wholistic living and care.	1	2	3	4	5	N/A
3.	I engage in wholistic practices to keep my mind, body and spirit well.	1	2	3	4	5	N/A
4.	The caregivers at Florida Hospital practice wholistic care.	1	2	3	4	5	N/A
5.	My entire health including mind, body and spirit are nurtured at Florida Hospital.	1	2	3	4	5	N/A
6.	I feel a sense of wholeness while working at Florida Hospital.	1	2	3	4	5	N/A

II. THE HEALING MINISTRY OF CHRIST – The mission of Florida Hospital is to extend the healing ministry of Christ. Therefore, Christian influences should be prevalent both in word, symbol, and practice. Practical applications would include prayer, spiritual nurturing, care, and compassion all motivated from the loving example of Jesus Christ.

1.	I understand what it means to extend the healing ministry of Christ.	1	2	3	4	5	N/A
2.	I believe that Christ provides an excellent model of compassionate care.	1	2	3	4	5	N/A
3.	I extend the healing ministry of Christ at Florida Hospital.	1	2	3	4	5	N/A
4.	I utilize prayer at Florida Hospital to extend the healing ministry of Christ.	1	2	3	4	5	N/A
5.	I sense a spirit of love and grace at Florida Hospital.	1	2	3	4	5	N/A
6.	I experience meaning from the mission of Florida Hospital.	1	2	3	4	5	N/A

III. HEALTH PRINCIPLES – From the earliest days of the Florida Sanitarium, a focus has been given to preventative health practices and education. The eight principles of health at the Florida Sanitarium were a nutritious diet, ample water consumption, regular exercise, plenty of fresh air, sufficient rest, appropriate use of sunlight, abstinence from harmful substances such as tobacco, and trusting relationships.

1.	I understand the health benefits of:						
	A. A nutritious diet	1	2	3	4	5	N/A
	B. Ample water consumption	1	2	3	4	5	N/A
	C. Regular exercise	1	2	3	4	5	N/A
	D. Fresh air	1	2	3	4	5	N/A
	E. Sufficient rest	1	2	3	4	5	N/A
	F. Appropriate use of sunlight	1	2	3	4	5	N/A
	G. Abstinence from harmful substances such as tobacco	1	2	3	4	5	N/A
	H. Trusting relationships	1	2	3	4	5	N/A

2.	I personally practice the following health principles:						
	A. A nutritious diet	1	2	3	4	5	N/A
	B. Ample water consumption	1	2	3	4	5	N/A
	C. Regular exercise	1	2	3	4	5	N/A
	D. Fresh air	1	2	3	4	5	N/A
	E. Sufficient rest	1	2	3	4	5	N/A
	F. Appropriate use of sunlight	1	2	3	4	5	N/A
	G. Abstinence from harmful substances such as tobacco	1	2	3	4	5	N/A
	H. Trusting relationships	1	2	3	4	5	N/A

IV. SEVENTH-DAY ADVENTIST BELIEFS – Florida Hospital is owned and operated by the Seventh-day Adventist Church and therefore the beliefs of the Church are to be honored. In addition to extending the loving and compassionate care as demonstrated by Christ, following all Biblical teachings including honoring Saturday as Sabbath are core to the Seventh-day Adventist belief system.

1.	Biblical teachings are cherished at Florida Hospital.	1	2	3	4	5	N/A
2.	Saturday (Sabbath) is a special day at Florida Hospital.	1	2	3	4	5	N/A
3.	Christian principles are practiced at Florida Hospital.	1	2	3	4	5	N/A
4.	I appreciate working for a faith-based hospital.	1	2	3	4	5	N/A
5.	I respect the Florida Hospital Seventh-day Adventist heritage.	1	2	3	4	5	N/A

V. IMAGE OF GOD – As reflected in Genesis, man and woman were created in the image of God. This means that all individuals are of great value regardless of their race, gender, or social status. Therefore, all individuals are treated as worthy and afforded the highest levels of dignity.

1.	I believe that every person is created in the image of God.	1	2	3	4	5	N/A
2.	Every person at Florida Hospital is valued regardless of race, gender or ability to pay.	1	2	3	4	5	N/A
3.	I treat others with respect because they are created in the image of God.	1	2	3	4	5	N/A
4.	The staff at Florida Hospital treats every individual as a child of God.	1	2	3	4	5	N/A
5.	I feel respected at Florida Hospital as a child of God.	1	2	3	4	5	N/A

VI. COMMUNITY – Florida Hospital was established as a community service to promote health and wholeness. Therefore, Florida Hospital should be actively engaged in the betterment of the health status of the community. In addition to the services provided in the hospital, these activities would include extended services such as community clinics and community events like blood drives, heart walks, backpacks for kids, and other community related initiatives.

1.	I believe that Florida Hospital has a positive relationship with the community.	1	2	3	4	5	N/A
2.	Florida Hospital is very interested in the health status of the community.	1	2	3	4	5	N/A
3.	I am personally engaged in community activities on behalf of Florida Hospital.	1	2	3	4	5	N/A
4.	I am involved with activities that improve the health status of the community.	1	2	3	4	5	N/A
5.	I feel a sense of belonging at Florida Hospital.	1	2	3	4	5	N/A
6.	I feel that it is important for Florida Hospital to be actively involved in the community.	1	2	3	4	5	N/A

VII. DEMOGRAPHIC DATA

A. Years of service at a Seventh-day Adventist healthcare institution including Florida Hospital:
   a. 0 – 9 Years
   b. 10 – 19 Years
   c. 20 – 29 Years
   d. 30 Years and greater

B. Religious Affiliation:
   a. Protestant Christian
   b. Seventh-day Adventist
   c. Roman Catholic
   d. Judaism
   e. Muslim
   f. Hindu
   g. None
   h. Other _____

Thank you for completing this survey and participating in this research.

NOTES

1   Gary Conner, *Six Sigma and Other Continuous Improvement Tools for the Small Shop* (Dearborn, MI: Society of Manufacturing Engineers, 2002), 62.

2   Jim C. Collins and Jerry I. Porras, *Built to Last* (New York: HarperCollins, 1994).

3   Jim C. Collins, "Building Companies to Last," *Inc.* (May 16, 1995), 83-84.

4   Collins and Porras, 73.

5   Ibid, 67.

6   Peter M. Senge, *The Fifth Disciple* (New York: Doubleday/Currency, 1990), 208.

7   Michael Fullan, *Leading in a Culture of Change* (San Francisco: Josey-Bass, 2001), xi.

8   Collins and Porras, 82.

9   Margatet J. Wheatley, *Leadership and the New Science* (San Francisco: Barrett-Koehler, 1999), 59.

10 Jim Collins, *Good to Great and the Social Sectors* (2005).

11 Kent Miller, "Competitive Strategies of Religious Organizations," *Strategic Management Journal* 23 (2002): 446.

12 Collins and Porras, 68.

13 Collins and Porras, 71.

14 Chun Wei Choo, *The Knowing Organization: How Organizations Use Information to Construct Meaning, Create Knowledge, and Make Decisions* (New York: Oxford University Press, 1998), 66.

15 James Burtchaell, *The Dying of the Light* (Grand Rapids, MI: William B. Eerdmans Publishing, 1998).

16 George Marsden, *The Soul of the American University: From Protestant Establishment to Established Nonbelief* (New York: Oxford University Press, 1994), 85.

17 Burtchaell, 823.

18 Burtchaell, 827.

19 Robert Benne, *Quality With Soul: How Six Premier Colleges and Universities Keep Faith With Their Religious Traditions* (Grand Rapids, MI: William B. Eerdmans, 2001), 28.

20 Marsden, 296.

21 Marsden, 265.

22 Burtchaell, 842.

23 Robert Sloan, "Baylor 2012: Ten-Year Vision 2002-2012," Baylor University (2002), *http://www.baylor.edu/vision/pdf/vision-full.pdf* (accessed July 10, 2005).

24 Benne, 19.

25 Benne, 45-46.

26 Leon Festinger, *A Theory of Cognitive Dissonance* (Stanford, CA: Stanford University Press, 1957).

27 Philip Selznik, *Leadership in Administration: A Sociological Interpretation* (Berkeley, CA: University of California Press, 1957), 17.

28 Selznik, 20.

29 Selznik, 63.

30 Karl E. Weick, *Sensemaking in Organizations* (Thousand Oaks, Ca: Sage, 1995).

31 Collins and Porras, 220.

32 Richard A. Schaefer, *Legacy: The Heritage of a Unique International Medical Outreach* (Mountain View, CA: Pacific Press, 1977).

33 Patsy Gerstner, *The Temple of Faith: A Pictorial History of the Battle Creek Sanitarium* (Unpublished manuscript, Springfield, IL, 1996): 3

34 Christine Oliver, "The Antecedents of Deinstitutionalization," *Organization Studies* 13 (1992): 564.

35 Ibid, 567.

ABOUT THE AUTHOR

RANDY HAFFNER, Ph.D., M.B.A. is a graduate of Walla Walla College in Washington and holds a Masters in Business Administration from the Roy E. Crummer Graduate School of Business at Rollins College in Winter Park, Florida. He received his Doctor of Philosophy degree in Leadership from Andrews University in Michigan.

Dr. Haffner currently serves as the Chief Executive Officer of Porter Adventist Hospital in Denver, Colorado. He also serves as President of the South Denver Group for Centura Health – a collection of hospitals including Porter, Littleton and Parker Adventist Hospital comprising about 700 licensed beds.

Prior to joining the Porter team, Dr. Haffner served as the Administrator of Florida Hospital Orlando in Orlando, Florida. In this role, he provided leadership and oversight for the operations of 1,081 inpatient beds and ancillary services. In addition, Dr. Haffner provided direct oversight for the Florida Hospital Cardiovascular Institute. Noteworthy projects he provided leadership for includes a $258 million 15-story bed tower, leading the Extending Excellence (Baldrige) journey and expanding the transplantation service.

Early in his career, Dr. Haffner served as the Chief Executive Officer of Volusia Medical Center in Orange City, Florida leading a joint venture new hospital with the West Volusia Hospital Authority.

As the youngest of four children born to a minister and a nurse, Dr. Haffner has nurtured a lifelong passion for faith-based healthcare and extending the healing ministry of Christ. Through his Baldrige interests, he is an advocate for balanced performance across the spectrum of healthcare including clinical results, service standards, team development, market growth and financial stewardship.

Dr. Haffner and his wife Cindy have three lovely daughters and make their home in Denver, where he is an avid runner, cyclist, mountain biker and snow skier.

For information about Dr. Haffner's speaking engagements, consulting opportunities, booking him as a speaker, or media interviews, please visit: FloridaHospitalPublishing.com.

Founded in 1930, Porter Adventist Hospital is known for its compassionate care and dedicated medical and nursing staff. Porter specializes in complex medicine, advanced cardiac services, cancer care and surgery. We offer centers for joint replacement, spine surgery and comprehensive cancer care. We also have a specialized head and neck surgery program, a leading transplant center and we offer cardiac services ranging from prevention to rehabilitation, including minimally invasive robotic heart surgery.

Porter Adventist Hospital Fast Facts:

- 2009: **Porter Adventist Hospital achieved Magnet™ designation for excellence in nursing services** by the American Nurses Credential Center's (ANCC) Magnet Recognition Program®.

- **Porter Adventist Hospital's Heart Institute** has been recognized as **one of the top programs in the country:**

    - 2010: HealthGrades — **Ranked No. 1 in Colorado for overall cardiac care** and in the top 10 percent nationally

    - 2008–2009: **Blue Distinction Center for Cardiac Care** by Blue Cross Blue Shield

    - 2008–2009: Cigna Healthcare **awarded Center of Excellence**

    - United Healthcare's **Cardiac Center of Excellence** designation

    - The Mercury Award for **Excellence in Cardiac Services** from the HCIA

    - **Recognition by the American Heart Association** for implementing AHA'S guidelines for cardiac care

- 2009: Porter was named a **Blue Distinction Center for Spine Surgery**

- 2009: Porter was named a **Blue Distinction Center for Knee and Hip Replacement**

- 2009: Received **designation from JCAHO as a Primary Stroke Center**

- 2009: **The Sleep Disorder Center at Porter Adventist Hospital received full accreditation** by the American Academy of Sleep Medicine.

- 2008: **Porter implemented a stroke alert program**, joined the Colorado Stroke Alliance and implemented American Heart Association/American Stroke Association Get with the Guidelines program.

Centura Health is Colorado's largest family of hospitals and health care services and one of the state's largest private employers, operating 12 hospitals, seven senior living communities and home care and hospice services.

Porter Adventist Hospital
✚ Centura Health.

porterhospital.org

FLORIDA HOSPITAL

The skill to heal. The spirit to care.

Florida Hospital Celebration Health

Florida Hospital Altamonte

GINSBURG

Florida Hospital Winter Park

Florida Hospital Orlando

Florida Hospital East Orlando

Florida Hospital Apopka

Florida Hospital Kissimmee

ABOUT FLORIDA HOSPITAL

For over one hundred years the mission of Florida Hospital has been: *To extend the health and healing ministry of Christ.* Opened in 1908, Florida Hospital is comprised of seven hospital campuses housing over 2,000 beds and eighteen walk-in medical centers. With over 16,000 employees—including 2,000 doctors and 4,000 nurses—Florida Hospital serves the residents and guests of Orlando, the No. 1 tourist destination in the world. Florida Hospital cares for over one million patients a year. Florida Hospital is a Christian, faith-based hospital that believes in providing Whole Person Care to all patients – mind, body and spirit.   Hospital fast facts include:

- **LARGEST ADMITTING HOSPITAL IN AMERICA.** Ranked No. 1 in the nation for inpatient admissions by the *American Hospital Association*.

- **AMERICA'S HEART HOSPITAL.** Ranked No. 1 in the nation for number of heart procedures performed each year, averaging 15,000 cases annually. MSNBC named Florida Hospital "America's Heart Hospital" for being the No. 1 hospital fighting America's No. 1 killer—heart disease.

- **HOSPITAL OF THE FUTURE.** At the turn of the century, the *Wall Street Journal* named Florida Hospital the "Hospital of the Future".

- **ONE OF AMERICA'S BEST HOSPITALS.** Recognized by *U.S. News & World Report* as "One of America's Best Hospitals" for ten years. Clinical specialties recognized have included: Cardiology, Orthopaedics, Neurology & Neurosurgery, Urology, Gynecology, Digestive Disorders, Hormonal Disorders, Kidney Disease, Ear, Nose & Throat and Endocrinology.

- **LEADER IN SENIOR CARE.** Florida Hospital serves the largest number of seniors in America through Medicare with a goal for each patient to experience a "Century of Health" by living to a healthy hundred.

- **TOP BIRTHING CENTER.** *Fit Pregnancy* magazine named Florida Hospital one of the "Top 10 Best Places in the Country to have a Baby". As a result, *The Discovery Health Channel* struck a three-year production deal with Florida Hospital to host a live broadcast called "Birth Day Live". Florida Hospital annually delivers over 9,000 babies.

- **CORPORATE ALLIANCES.** Florida Hospital maintains corporate alliance relationships with a select group of Fortune 500 companies including Disney, Nike, Johnson & Johnson, Philips, AGFA, and Stryker.

- **DISNEY PARTNERSHIP.** Florida Hospital is the Central Florida health & wellness resource of the *Walt Disney World* ® Resort. Florida Hospital also partnered with Disney to build the ground breaking health and wellness facility called Florida Hospital Celebration Health located in Disney's town of Celebration, Florida. Disney and Florida Hospital recently partnered to build a new state-of-the-art Children's Hospital.

- **HOSPITAL OF THE 21ST CENTURY.** Florida Hospital Celebration Health was awarded the *Premier Patient Services Innovator Award* as "The Model for Healthcare Delivery in the 21st Century".

- **SPORTS EXPERTS.** Florida Hospital is the official hospital of the Orlando *Magic* NBA basketball team. In addition, Florida Hospital has an enduring track record of providing exclusive medical care to many sports organizations. These organizations have included: Disney's Wide World of Sports, Walt Disney World's Marathon Weekend, the Capital One Bowl, and University of Central Florida Athletics. Florida Hospital has also provided comprehensive healthcare services for the World Cup and Olympics.

- **PRINT RECOGNITION.** Self magazine named Florida Hospital one of America's "Top 10 Hospitals for Women". *Modern Healthcare* magazine proclaimed it one of America's best hospitals for cardiac care.

- **CONSUMER CHOICE AWARD WINNER.** Florida Hospital has received the Consumer Choice Award from the *National Research Corporation* every year from 1996 to the present.

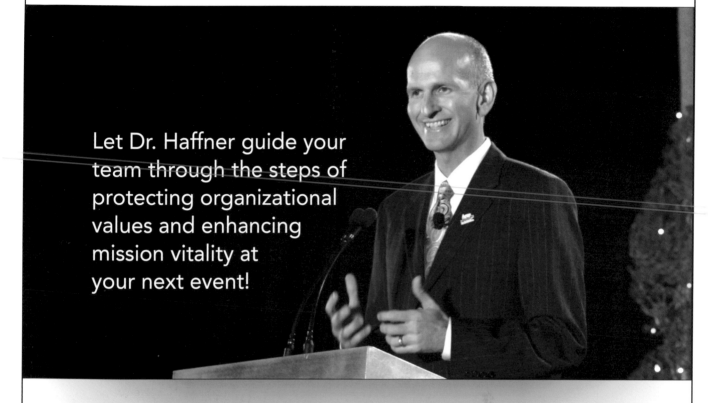